MSMEs, Let's Go Digital?

Doubts to Digital: From Apprehension to Action

Beyond dashboards. Beyond rhetoric. Into reality.

Piyush Singh

For permission requests, write to the author at:

contactpiyushsingh@gmail.com

ISBN (Paperback): 978-93-344-2336-5

ISBN (Digital, eBook): 978-93-344-3012-7

Published by Piyush Singh

Delhi, India

First Edition

Printed and bound in India

MSMEs, Let's Go Digital?

Acknowledgements

Every meaningful journey is built on collective strength. This book is no exception. Behind every page lies the encouragement of my family, the trust of colleagues and friends, the resilience of entrepreneurs I have met, and the guidance of faith and mentors who inspired me to keep moving forward.

I am deeply grateful to my parents, wife, children, and employees for their patience and unwavering belief in my dream. They stood by me through the uncertainties of building and scaling both for-profit and not-for-profit ventures, bearing with my mistakes, experiments.

A special note of gratitude to the countless Nano, Micro, Small, and Medium Enterprises (MSMEs) who generously shared their stories, challenges, and aspirations with me, whether on streets, shops or in their lovely, well-designed cabins across India, that is Bharat. Their honesty, resilience, and warmth have been my greatest teachers.

I thank my mentors, colleagues, seniors, editing team, friends, and industry peers who supported me, challenged me, guided me, and trusted me with opportunities, even in difficult times. Their encouragement helped me to visualise and come up with this book on M-SME digitalisation.

Finally, I acknowledge the tireless efforts of all stakeholders involved in building and improving the MSME ecosystem, government, ministries, government bodies, NGOs, industry associations, philanthropic organisations, multilaterals, financial institutions, technology service providers, and consultants. Their policies, innovations, and collective effort continue to create an environment that enables entrepreneurs to thrive.

To all of you who have contributed in ways big or small: this book carries a part of your spirit.

Table of Contents

Preface

I am an entrepreneur in the FinTech and Nano, MSME digitalisation domain. This book reflects my extensive interactions working with nano, micro, small, and medium enterprises (MSMEs) across both urban and rural India. The book has been shaped not in isolation, but in the everyday spaces where businesses thrive and struggle, such as street vendors, kirana shops, factory floors, warehouses, and family-run enterprises, those of both legacy and first-time entrepreneurs.

Having built and managed multiple enterprises in both for-profit and not-for-profit domains, I deeply relate to the dilemmas, apprehensions, and aspirations of business owners. The challenges that consultants and implementation agencies face in discussing and convincing Nano and MSME businesses to learn, adopt, and scale with digital solutions.

For my work, I regularly interact with many nano and MSMEs across the country and various sectors to understand their digital challenges. Many of the stories and insights in this book are drawn from those journeys, digital struggles, and my consultancy and implementation work across the country.

Why This Book

The challenges Nano and MSMEs face are wide-ranging and complex, and no single book can capture them all. That is why I have chosen to focus specifically on digitalisation and digital transformation, areas where I specialise, and where change is both inevitable and often intimidating, especially at the conjunction of shifting behaviour and adopting technology.

It's the book that voices what MSME owners are too hesitant to ask in public, and answers them honestly, with practical steps they can use at any stage of their journey.

This book is a collection of 43 real apprehensions voiced by MSMEs whenever they hear, attempt, or adopt digital. I have encountered, observed, managed, and personally faced these issues during years of fieldwork, consultancy, and my own businesses. All the names of individuals, businesses and locations have been changed for confidentiality, but the experiences remain authentic and relatable.

These are not abstract theories or prescriptive models. They are grounded reflections of how MSMEs perceive digitalisation:

- Sometimes with curiosity,
- Often with caution,
- And frequently with hesitation.

Each chapter is structured as a story of behaviour and digitalisation, illustrating not only the technical concerns but also the cultural, emotional, and generational factors at play.

Who This Book Is For

This book is intended as a resource for a broad spectrum of readers:

- MSMEs seeking clarity and confidence on digitalisation.
- Academicians, consultants, NGOs, and service providers aiming to understand the real barriers MSMEs face. A tool for the ecosystem.
- Financial institutions and policymakers who want to design more inclusive strategies for digital adoption, and understand the apprehensions to address.
- A solution service provider who is trying to build a digital product or software for MSMEs

If you are any one of the above and trying to convince MSMEs to go digital, and they share with you one or more of the apprehensions mentioned in the book. Gift this book to them, or recommend it. They will be able to understand the point in a story and case study format that is closer and relatable to them.

The focus is deliberately on businesses that have endured shifting policies, economic pressures, and waves of technological change, yet remain cautious about adopting digital. This book does not focus on enterprises that are already digitally advanced, but on those that want to, or are yet to, step onto the digital path.

What This Book Offers

By compiling these 43 apprehensions, the book seeks to:

- Highlight why many enterprises hesitate to adopt digital tools.
- Unveil subtle but critical barriers such as generational conflicts, fear of failure, resistance to change, and status quo biases.
- Provide a safe, respectful space for MSMEs to explore digitalisation at their own pace and on their own terms.

This is not a technical manual or promotional guide. It is a human-centred playbook, pragmatic, compassionate, and designed from the bottom up, based on lived experiences rather than external mandates.

How to Engage with This Book

There is no single prescribed way to navigate these chapters. Readers may:

- Read sequentially to follow the progression of reflections.
- Explore individual chapters as stand-alone insights for team discussions or peer learning.
- Use the book as a reference and companion for training programs, community workshops, or policy dialogues.

- Share relevant chapters with MSME entrepreneurs who are exploring digital adoption.
- Gift the book or recommend it to entrepreneurs as part of your Digital Skilling Program, who may need to learn and understand the digital journey from apprehension to confidence.

Closing Note

Digitalisation is often presented as a one-way street. In reality, it is a nuanced, personal journey. The aim of this book is not to convince or coerce, but to help transform confusion into clarity and hesitation into informed action.

Change need not happen all at once. It can begin with a single step, a single story, or one tool that fits your context. Digitalisation, at its core, is not about technology alone; it is about people, their aspirations, and their ability to adapt.

This book is dedicated to them.

Piyush Singh

Delhi, India

contactpiyushsingh@gmail.com

Section 1: The Fear & Resistance

Every big change begins with resistance. MSMEs in India have long relied on tried-and-tested methods passed down over generations. When "digital" enters the conversation, the first instinct is often fear, fear of losing jobs, fear of losing control, fear of being laughed at by elders, or simply the comfort of doing things the "real" way with pen, paper, and personal trust. This section highlights these emotional and cultural barriers so we can see them clearly and gradually begin to dismantle them.

Chapter 1: "When Survival Feels Like a Full-Time Job: Can Digital Still Help?"

"The secret of change is to focus all your energy not on fighting the old, but on building the new."

— *Socrates*

Its late afternoon in Patna, and the sun is still blazing down. The streets are alive with noise, and I find myself waiting outside a little vegetable shop nestled at the corner of a busy residential lane. This shop is more of a makeshift structure, crafted from wood and cloth, filled with crates of potatoes, onions, and whatever seasonal vegetables are in stock.

Behind the counter, there's Mr. Ajay Kumar, a lean man of 45, dressed in a well-worn cotton kurta. He wipes his forehead, not out of stress, but from the familiar routine of someone who hasn't taken a break in hours. Next to him, his daughter Anu, around 19, perches on a stool, helping to tally up some payments in a battered notebook.

This is my second visit.

"Sir, it's hard enough to make ends meet— and you're talking about technology? Every day, I don't know if I'll make ₹500 or ₹5. But you want me to use some app to plan for next year?" he had replied, his tone polite but resistant.

Today, I've come with a bit more patience and less pitch.

The Core Hesitation

Once the rush dies down, we settle onto plastic stools behind the shop.

I start gently, "How are you, Ajay ji?"

He offers a brief smile. 'Just surviving, sir.' *If the vegetables sell, it's okay. Sometimes they do, sometimes they don't. The rains affect it, rising prices affect it, and on top of that, people who owe me money switch off their phones and disappear.*"

And there it was.

His reluctance towards digital wasn't just about technology; it was rooted in survival anxiety. When every day is a gamble, "future planning" feels like a luxury.

So when I brought up digital tools again, he was cautious, even a bit irritated.

"Ajay ji, I understand that every day feels like survival. But think of it this way: digital tools aren't a luxury anymore; they are your shield against uncertainty. Just like a weighing scale helps you measure correctly, digital tools help you track, remind, and recover money more effectively.

You said some customers switch off their phones when they owe you money. But what if, instead of chasing them, an automatic message reminds them every few days—politely but persistently? What if Anu can see at a glance who owes what, and for how long?

You don't need to do everything. But even a small digital step, like tracking udhaar in an app or reminding customers through

14

WhatsApp, can protect the business you've built with sweat and grit. Going digital isn't about changing your business, it's about strengthening it so that survival becomes stability, and one day, growth."

"Look, sir, we wake up thinking of whether there will be sales today. These apps are designed for individuals who have both money and time. We small people are only trying"

He wasn't dismissing me; he was being real.

The Engagement & Exploration

I nodded—not in agreement, but out of respect for where he stood. I wasn't there to sell him a solution. I was there to co-think with him about his everyday challenges and what might help him.

A few days later, I received a missed call from Ajay ji. When I called back, it was his daughter Anu who answered. "Papa said to call you. He wants to see that app again. We've decided to try it for a week."

When I returned to the shop, the familiar notebook was still there—but now, beside it, Anu was entering daily udhaar into the app. She had even sent their first payment reminder.

Ajay ji looked amused. "I didn't get any money yet," he said, chuckling. "But the customer called and said, 'Just remembered, brother, will come and give it tomorrow. That counts for something, right?" Ajay ji glanced sideways at Anu, a mix of curiosity and cautious hope softening his otherwise tired face.

No one had gone fully digital overnight—but something meaningful had changed. From refusal, they had moved to curiosity. And that, for many, is where fundamental transformation begins.

I reminded him that this small step wasn't just about going digital; it was about taking control of his business and his future, one rupee at a time.

Framework: Survive → Sustain → Scale

At the end of our session, I sketched a simple three-step ladder for him on a scrap of paper. If you meet someone like Ajay Ji and want to help them, use the model below.

SURVIVE

- Use a digital ledger to keep track of credit.
- Send reminders.
- Identify your loyal customers.

SUSTAIN

- Monitor daily sales trends.
- Figure out which products sell quickly and which don't.
- Use WhatsApp Business to keep frequent buyers updated.

SCALE

- Start accepting digital payments.
- Request online reviews from satisfied customers.
- Consider offering seasonal promotions via SMS or WhatsApp.

"None of this has to happen in a year; you can start implementing it week by week," I said.

Ajay ji nodded. "We used to live by our ways, but now we'll try new methods."

Closing Reflection

This chapter isn't about a breakthrough; it's about honouring the beginning.

For countless MSMEs, the thought of going digital feels like scaling Mount Everest: daunting, distant, and risky.

But what if we viewed it as taking one small step toward gaining clarity in your business?

Not to impress anyone. Not to unthinkingly "modernise."

But to help you stay afloat, stay sharp, and maintain control.

That's what Ajay ji did.

And that's what you can do too, whenever you're ready.

No pressure.

Just a possibility. This chapter isn't about instant transformation. It's about honouring the courage to take the first step, even when the ground beneath feels shaky."

Chapter 2: The Way We Have Always Done It

"Change is hardest at the beginning, messiest in the middle and best at the end."

— *Robin Sharma*

It was around 11:15 a.m. when I reached the outskirts of Nagpur, to a site operated by a second-generation construction firm specialising in residential and commercial projects across Vidarbha. Their temporary site office, a rusted container with an attached fan, sat wedged between stacks of red bricks and a mixing machine churning like a sleepy tiger.

Inside, I met Amritlal Deshmukh. In his late fifties, tall, deeply tanned, with white cement lining his fingernails, he had the look of someone who trusted hands-on wisdom more than any dashboard. He offered tea from a steel flask and said, "We make it fresh. These packet ones are all water."

Once seated, he said what many others had said before, but with more composure than complaint. "People like us? We've built half this city without apps or QR codes. And now every second person walks in saying we must go digital and change our systems."

"But tell me this," he continued, "did any of these software engineers ever walk barefoot on wet concrete to fix a slab before rain?"

This was not resistance. It was earned pride.

The Mindset Behind the Method

I asked him how he tracked site needs.

"Simple," he said. "Every site supervisor calls me by 6:30 p.m. I note it down, total it, and the next morning we arrange deliveries."

"And if something is missed or under-calculated?" I asked.

"Then we manage. Send a tempo, shift some stock from another site. It's part of the job."

"What if you could avoid just one of those emergencies a week?" I asked.

He looked unconvinced. "By using what? Some expensive app?"

"No," I said. "By using a simple sheet and voice note."

A New Way, Rooted in Old Wisdom

I told him about another contractor nearby who had not changed much either, except that every evening, his supervisor filled a basic WhatsApp form noting what was used and what was needed for the next three days.

"Same people, same phones, just a small habit," I explained. "The owner now sees shortages two days in advance, places bulk orders once a week, and avoids last-minute supplier overcharges."

"And it's not just him," I said. "There's a lady in Coimbatore who runs a tile showroom. Small business. Just five people. She trained her delivery guy to record voice memos for incoming stock. Now she knows exactly when to reorder and never runs out of inventory."

Amritlal ji looked surprised. "A woman running this kind of business?"

"Yes," I smiled. "And she's been doing it for fifteen years. Only recently tried a change, and it's made her job easier, not harder."

Mr. Deshmukh raised his eyebrows. "And it works?"

"He says it saved him thousands of rupees in logistics last month alone."

The Trial that Shifted Something

Amritlal ji didn't respond with a yes or no. He said, "Let me think," and turned to watch a worker stacking bricks at the far end of the site.

The next morning, I got a brief call. "Come again tomorrow. My nephew and supervisor will be here. I want them to hear this, too."

When I arrived, the three of them were already in discussion. The supervisor looked a little unsure, the nephew was cautiously curious, and Amritlal ji was listening without interrupting. I repeated the same suggestion: begin with a straightforward step. No software. Just regular updates on stock movement.

The supervisor was the first to react. "Sir, we are already stretched. Sometimes I forget to send even the attendance. This will be extra pressure."

The nephew added, "And what if the internet does not work or someone puts in the wrong quantity? Who checks?"

Amritlal ji nodded, then turned to me. "This is what I am worried about. We may start something but leave it halfway. I am not against change, but it must last."

I suggested starting with just five days of trial. Nothing formal. Simply a tracker with a normal voice note every evening with three points: what was used, what is running low, and what is needed.

They agreed to try.

For the first few days, messages came in. Sometimes late. Sometimes incomplete. One day, it was just a photo of an empty cement sack with no caption. Another time, it was a list scribbled on paper that was clicked on hurriedly. But something was better than nothing.

On the sixth day, there was no update.

The next morning, an urgent order had to be placed for binding wire. The delivery cost was higher than usual. When I met Amritlal ji later that week, he said quietly, "We tried, but I feel we're only half ready."

I replied, "Maybe it is not the idea, but the tool. A message can be missed. What if you used a small form instead? Same questions, but in a format that stays recorded."

Over the next week, his nephew explored a few options. They contacted two digital support vendors, one of whom quoted a high package for a multi-site rollout. The other, a local tech advisor, offered to customise a basic Google Form in the local language. He promised to train the team, help them tweak it as needed, and charge a reasonable monthly fee for support.

In parallel, they also reached out to two fellow contractors from other regions. One from Pune had tried a costly ERP system and discontinued it. Another from Guwahati used a simple daily log and claimed it helped him plan better. That was the example that resonated most with Amritlal ji.

By the second week, they had built a basic form with dropdowns, voice input, and auto-recording of entries. It took under two minutes to fill.

A few days later, the form caught an early drop in sand stock. The nephew added it to the bulk dispatch without anyone needing to raise a panic.

That evening, I got a message: "Now I see it. We are not replacing our way. We are just catching our mistakes earlier."

The confidence was not because of technology. It came from testing the unknown, one step at a time, with help they trusted.

Reflection

While reflecting on the entire episode, I noticed a trend that any MSME undergoes whenever it experiences a change; more than financial concerns, it's mostly the emotional aspect and resistance. I can relate to such organisational change, as I have been part of many organisations and witnessed similar responses. I have also experienced similar situations within my organisation and with other clients; it's just that I am now aware of this, hence it passes quickly.

It's called "The Change Curve", "Kubler-Ross Model in Business" by Elisabeth Kübler-Ross. Any organisational or personal change goes through these Seven stages –

Shock → Denial → Anger → Bargaining → Depression → Acceptance → Integration

And long-term sustainable change can only happen if the integration stage becomes the new norm and standard.

This gets repeated for each change, and as **Kurt Lewin** in his Change Management Model states:

Unfreeze – Prepare for change, **Change** – Implement new processes, **Refreeze** – Institutionalise new behaviour

Deshmukh ji did not change his project manager or buy a fancy ERP system. He simply added one small layer of visibility to his old system, shifted and adjusted his mindset, and he got it. Change is painful and is the most critical part of any digital transformation process.

Sometimes, the best way to protect tradition is not to keep it hidden but to let it evolve, one form at a time.

And I've seen this happen even in micro-setups, like a small bakery in Varanasi run by three staff members, who transitioned from a handwritten notebook to a shared Google Sheet for order tracking. Change isn't about scale. It's about willingness.

Chapter 3: The Human Side of Going Digital

"It is not the strongest of the species that survive, nor the most intelligent, but the one most responsive to change."

— *Charles Darwin*

It was around noon when I met Suresh Mittal ji in his office, tucked behind rows of godowns and bustling lanes in Gandhinagar, Delhi. His business is massive by any standard: hundreds of fabric varieties, legacy supplier networks across Surat and Ludhiana, and turnover figures that would impress any banker. But what impressed me more was something else: his sharp eye for detail. He didn't look at his phone once during our entire conversation, an authoritarian feat that is particularly challenging in the age of constant noise and digital media distractions. Every call, every entry, every dispatch, he asked his staff, confirmed mentally, and approved with clockwork precision.

Over tea, I brought up digitalisation.

He looked at me through his golden-framed glasses, a look that I could not decipher, annoyed, sarcastic, or just saying not again. "You consultants keep coming and saying, 'Go digital, go digital.' But let me ask you, what happens to the twenty boys who run this business with me? Who handles ledger books, delivery slips, gate pass registers, and inventory? If I replace all this with an app, what will they do? Watch?"

This wasn't resistance. It was stewardship.

"Mittal ji," I replied, "I would have said the same in your position. You've built this with people, not platforms. You've taken care of those boys, some of whom you probably hired before they even knew how to read invoice numbers properly. But may I ask you something?"

He nodded.

When Mindsets Change, Models Evolve

"You remember the days when you didn't take online payments?" I asked.

He smiled. "Of course. We'd lose sleep every time a cheque bounced."

"And now?"

"Now, even our Ludhiana suppliers prefer UPI and Net Banking payment, and GST has also changed things a lot."

"Exactly. You didn't adopt it because it was fashionable; you did it when it made your business safer."

That's the point. It's not about 'being digital'. It's about knowing when to pivot because your business deserves better tools.

I continued, "Just like you took a chance then, you'll have to consider doing it again, only this time, not to replace people, but to equip them."

He leaned forward. "But most of my staff isn't ready. Half of them don't even have email IDs."

"Were they ready to manage a 100-cr operation when they first joined you?" I asked. "You made them ready. You trained, taught, and trusted them. And they rose. You've done this before, Suresh ji.

Digital is just another version of the same story. A new skill, same principle."

Why It's Not About Losing Jobs But Elevating Roles

I took out my notebook and drew four boxes.

Observe → Assist → Own → Guide

"That's your hierarchy already, right?" I said. "A new worker observes. He then assists with loading rolls and checking invoices. Slowly, he begins to own tasks. Finally, he teaches others."

He nodded.

"What if you introduced a basic stock-tracking app, not to replace your guy at Gate 3, but to make sure *he* starts managing stock mismatch issues digitally? His role expands, not shrinks. And maybe he gets the confidence to handle customer queries next. You don't cut people. You upgrade them."

He was listening now, not out of courtesy but curiosity.

Evidence from His Evolution

"You know what's funny?" he said. "When my son came back from college and started selling dead stock on Instagram, I thought he was wasting time. But some of those orders now bring in more margin than bulk supply."

"There you go," I said. "Digital didn't remove your core business; it extended it. You didn't stop selling to retailers. You added a channel."

The Thought That Turned the Tide

"So what are you saying?" he asked. "I hire someone to digitise, or I train my boys?"

"Both. Start with one. Let one junior track incoming inventory digitally. Not to replace the accountant, but to flag gaps earlier. Let someone else handle online queries. Bit by bit. Business continuity with future-readiness."

I left him with one sentence that stayed with him: "The job of a good owner is not to resist change, but to make sure his people don't get left behind when change happens."

Three weeks later, I got a voice note from him.

"That young fellow Ramesh, who barely spoke in meetings, is now managing stock alerts on his phone. We discovered a significant dispatch discrepancy that we'd have otherwise missed. That, too, before it left the warehouse. Maybe this digital thing isn't so bad after all."

Reflection

The fear that digitalisation will take away jobs is valid. It often comes from seeing abrupt, top-down tech adoption that pushes people out before pulling them up. But it doesn't have to be that way.

What we need is not digital replacement but digital role expansion, helping people become *more*, not *less*.

Suresh Mittal ji didn't transform his business overnight. He just let one staffer become a little more skilled and confident.

And sometimes, in businesses built on trust and tradition, one shift in the role is all it takes to shift the mindset of the whole organisation.

Role Expansion Ladder in a Fabric Trading Business

Stage	Who Tries It	What Changes
Observe	New staff, the dispatch boys	Watches how physical stock is managed, learns traditional process flow
Assist	Junior stock handlers	Starts using barcode scanners or app input for incoming inventory
Own	Inventory lead, gate manager	Tracks stock discrepancies, generates reports digitally
Guide	Senior operations staff	Mentors juniors in hybrid (manual + digital) systems, handles analytics

Closing Thought

In industries where legacy and livelihoods are closely tied together, digital transformation doesn't need to disrupt. It needs to be dignified.

And the businesses that will lead tomorrow are not the ones that went digital first. They're the ones who took their people along.

Chapter 4: The Cost of Reputation

"It is not the strongest of the species that survive, nor the most intelligent, but the one most responsive to change."

- *Charles Darwin*

In the heart of Lucknow, nestled between a bustling market and a quiet residential street, stood Navoday Coaching Classes. The building was old, its walls marked with faded posters of past academic triumphs. Inside, the air was thick with the scent of old paper and chalk dust. This was the domain of Mr. Ved Prakash, a man in his late 50s, a teacher by trade, and a traditionalist by conviction. He believed in the power of a blackboard, a personal touch, and the unwritten promise of a student's success. For him, the business was not about numbers on a spreadsheet, but about the bonds forged between a mentor and a student. His reputation was his currency, built over thirty years of tireless work and countless success stories that spread through the city by word of mouth.

I met him in his small office, a sanctuary of books and framed photographs of his top-performing students. He gestured to the photos with a hint of pride. "Our reputation is our marketing," he said with a serene smile. "A fancy website, social media posts, all of that is just noise. It's impersonal. A student's success story, told by a parent to another parent over a cup of tea, is worth more than any thousand-rupee ad. I don't want to become a faceless, digital brand. I want to look my students in the eye and teach them. Going digital means a lot of changes and new things, and frankly, I don't want that."

His apprehension was not a rejection of progress, but a fierce protection of his core values. He saw the digital world as a threat to the authenticity of his brand, a force that would cheapen his personal touch and replace it with a cold, transactional exchange. He believed his business was an island of purity in a sea of commercialism, and he was content to keep it that way. His enrolment was stable, his reputation was sound, and he felt no need to change a system that had worked for so long.

The Invisible Threat: A Reputation Unseen

The problem with Mr. Prakash's conviction was that the world outside his classroom was changing, and his reputation was no longer reaching the people who needed to hear it. The invisible threat arrived in the form of a new, aggressive competitor. A major ed-tech company, with a slick and well-funded marketing campaign, established a regional office in the city. Their ads were everywhere: on social media feeds, in newspapers, and on YouTube videos. They promised a "digital-first" experience with animated lectures, interactive apps, and personalised dashboards. They spoke the language of the new generation of students and, more importantly, of their tech-savvy parents.

Mr. Prakash's enrolment, while not declining, had completely stopped growing. He was losing the battle for visibility and relevance. A relentless wave of polished, commercial content was drowning out his years of success stories. Google searches were replacing the conversations over tea. He would hear parents say, "We saw this new company online, and their videos look so professional." His own website, a relic from the early 2000s, was stagnant, and his social media presence was nonexistent. He was a master of his craft, but to the new market, he was invisible.

The painful reality was laid bare one evening when his daughter, Ananya, a young professional who was well-versed in the digital world, sat him down with her laptop. She showed him the stark contrast. On one screen was his competitor's website, a masterpiece of modern design with glowing testimonials and professional videos. On the other hand, there was his own. The comparison was devastating. He saw, for the first time, that the excellence he had poured his life into was not being communicated to the world in a way it understood. His reputation was not gone; it was simply unseen. The very chaos he had tried to avoid had found a way to hurt his business from the outside, and he had no platform to fight back.

The New Outlook: Digital as an Amplifier

The solution wasn't for Mr. Prakash to hire a large, expensive marketing team that would betray his values. The solution was to use a simple, elegant tool that would allow him to do what he had always done: to tell a story, but on a much larger scale. Ananya introduced him to a Generative AI content platform, presenting it not as a replacement for his personal touch but as an amplifier for his authentic voice.

"This," she explained, gesturing to the clean interface, "isn't about a machine creating a new brand for you. It's about a machine helping you share the brand you already have. You provide the heart, the stories, and the AI provides the voice and the reach."

She gave him a simple demonstration. "Tell me about Ravi, your top student who scored 98%." Mr. Prakash, with his hands gesturing, told a heartfelt story of Ravi's hard work, his struggles, and his final success. Ananya typed a few notes into the platform. Within seconds, the AI generated three polished pieces of content: a succinct tweet, a longer Facebook post with a powerful call-to-action, and a professional, heartfelt blog post ready to be published on their website.

Mr. Prakash was stunned. The content was professional, but the core of the story, the authenticity, the emotion, the personal touch, was all his. The AI had simply translated his raw experience into a format that resonated with a modern audience. It wasn't a faceless, impersonal tool; it was an assistant that understood his brand's soul.

The mindset shift was immediate and profound. He realised the AI was not a threat to his reputation; it was a guardian. He was no longer just a local teacher; he was a mentor whose methods could inspire students across the city and beyond. He started providing the "prompts" himself, sharing anecdotes, study tips, and motivational quotes from his decades of experience. The AI turned them into daily, compelling content.

From Invisible to Irresistible

The results of this transformation were remarkable. Within a few months, Navoday Coaching Classes' digital presence was vibrant and authentic.

- Expanded Reach: The website, now regularly updated with fresh, engaging blog posts, began to show up in online searches. Their social media pages, once dormant, became a hub of student success stories and valuable content. Parents who had never heard of them now saw their expertise and their genuine care for students.

- Brand Promise: The ability to communicate directly with the public allowed them to build a powerful brand narrative that stood out from the generic, impersonal marketing of the ed-tech giants. They were not just selling a course; they were selling a proven method and a personal relationship.

- Sustainable Growth: Enrollment didn't just stabilise; it began to grow steadily. The new students weren't just looking for the cheapest option; they were looking for a brand they trusted, a story they connected with. The AI-powered content had become their most powerful marketing asset.

Mr. Prakash, once a staunch opponent of the digital world, now sees it as an essential part of his business. The mindset shift from rejection to acceptance was the most critical transformation. He learned that the digital world is not a substitute for authenticity; it is the most powerful tool ever created to amplify it. The very changes he feared were the ones that made his business more resilient and more relevant than ever before.

Mini-Framework: The Mindset Shift from Traditional to Digital

- The Problem is External, Not Internal: Recognise that not being digital doesn't protect you from it; it just makes you vulnerable to its external forces. The threat is not in your business but in the marketplace.

- Digital as an Amplifier, Not a Replacement: Change your view of digital tools. They are not here to replace your core values or personal touch. They are here to amplify them, to extend your reach, and to share your story with a new generation.

- The Power of Authenticity: In a world of polished, commercial content, authenticity is the most valuable currency. Your unique story and genuine experience are your most powerful marketing assets.

- Embrace the New Language: Learn to speak the digital language. This doesn't mean becoming a marketer; it means using digital tools to translate your authentic voice into the formats that resonate with your target audience.

Reflection

Mr. Ved Prakash's journey is a classic case study in the necessity of a mindset shift in the face of modern challenges. His initial resistance was rooted in a noble place: a desire to protect his brand's integrity. But in today's world, a brand's integrity must be communicated as well as lived. He learned that the digital world is not an abstract concept; it's the new public square. And to thrive, you must be present and you must be heard. The transformation was not in his teaching methods, but in his approach to sharing them.

The AI didn't make his teaching better; it made his reputation visible. It didn't make his brand more authentic; it simply allowed him to prove it. The mindset shift from fearing change to embracing it as a tool for amplification was the key to his business's survival and future growth.

Chapter 5: More Than Just a Fancy Distraction

"Progress is impossible without change, and those who cannot change their minds cannot change anything."

- *George Bernard Shaw*

In Bhagalpur, Bihar, small weaving units remain the backbone of the local economy. The town is renowned for its silk, but the industry is fragmented into hundreds of micro and small workshops that heavily rely on middlemen, wholesalers, and traders in larger cities. Many units still function in courtyards with a handful of looms, where family members manage production, sales, and accounts.

Rafiq Ahmad runs one such unit. His workshop has six looms and ten weavers, most of them relatives or neighbours. The products are of high quality and in demand, but like many others, he sells mainly through mandi traders and personal contacts. The idea of putting his work online makes him uncomfortable.

He explained his hesitation to me directly. "Sir, I don't want my competitors to see me struggle online. If I post something and there are no orders, or if I post low-quality photos, people will laugh. In the mandi, if I don't sell on a given day, no one outside knows. But online, everyone will see my failure."

Before I could respond, his father, who is retired but still influential in decisions, added firmly, "This online business is a distraction. Our forefathers never needed it. They built respect through patience and quality, not by posting pictures on phones. These are new-age fancies. Real buyers come through hard work and relationships, not through screens."

Rafiq lowered his eyes. He respected his father deeply, but the generational clash was visible. He wanted to try, but he also feared ridicule and the burden of expectations.

The Fear of Public Struggle

Rafiq's fear is not unusual. In traditional markets, failure remains a private matter. If a trader does not sell, it is known only to a few peers. Online, every ignored post or unanswered listing feels like public humiliation. Business owners equate visibility with vulnerability.

I asked Rafiq a simple question. "Do you remember your first days of weaving? Did you make perfect cloth immediately?"

He smiled faintly. "No. I ruined several pieces before I made one that could be sold."

"And did the whole city see those mistakes?"

He shook his head. "Only my family knew."

"Exactly," I said. "Every skill looks awkward in the beginning. People remember the finished product, not the failed attempts. Online presence is the same. Your first posts may not get attention, but the later ones will. Competitors will not remember your early mistakes. Customers will only remember the fabric they buy."

His father still objected. "Weaving is real. It can be touched and felt. This internet is not real. It is an illusion."

Reminders of Past Change

I turned to him with respect. "Chacha ji, do you remember when payments shifted from only cash to cheques to digital? At that time, many traders considered cheques and digital payments to be unreliable. They said real money is only coins in hand. But today, everyone accepts transfers. That was not an illusion. That was survival."

The father looked at me, silent. The example had touched a memory.

Rafiq added, "Abba, you also said once that machine looms would never work, that only handlooms would survive. However, today, half of our production is automated by machines. If we had refused then, we would have closed the business."

The father leaned back. His silence spoke more than his words. He had resisted before, and then adapted.

The Burden of Respect

Rafiq looked at me again, his voice lower. "The truth is that I am not only worried about competitors. I am worried about respect. If I try online and nothing happens, people will laugh at me. Elders will say I wasted time. Relatives will gossip. In our town, one mistake becomes a permanent label. I do not want that weight."

His father gave a slight nod. He understood this fear, too. In business families, reputation often takes precedence over profit in the short term.

I said, "Every new practice feels like a gamble in the beginning. However, remember that your elders also faced ridicule when they made changes in their time. Over time, those same changes became the new normal. What feels like risk today may become routine tomorrow."

The father smiled reluctantly. "When I first started selling directly to Delhi buyers instead of through middlemen, people mocked me. They said I was breaking tradition. Now everyone does the same. At that time, they called me arrogant. Later, they copied me."

Rafiq looked at his father with new confidence. The room felt lighter.

A Small Test

To move the discussion from debate to action, I asked Rafiq to bring one of his best scarves. He showed me a piece dyed in indigo with a gold border. I clicked a simple photo with the loom in the background and suggested, "Let us just send this on WhatsApp to your known buyers. Not to the public. Only to those who already deal with you. Think of it as sending a sample, nothing more."

Rafiq hesitated but agreed. Within an hour, one of his Delhi contacts replied with an order for six pieces.

Rafiq's eyes widened. His father leaned forward in surprise. The hesitation in the room gave way to quiet acknowledgement.

"This is not begging online," I said. "This is the same as hanging your best fabric at the front of your mandi stall. It is simply a new doorway."

That evening, Rafiq shared another concern. "If I post my designs, competitors will copy them."

His father agreed quickly. "Yes, they will. They always do."

I explained, "But they already copied in the mandi. They walk through your stall and take notes. At least online, you have a record of who posted first. It becomes proof of originality."

Rafiq thought for a while. "So maybe posting is not a weakness. Maybe it is also a kind of protection."

The father did not reply, but he no longer dismissed the idea.

Mini Framework: How to Shift Mindset and Approach

1. **Remember past adaptations.** Every generation resisted change once, from cheques to machines. Change is not betrayal; it is continuity.

2. **Start with a safe circle.** Share products with existing buyers first before posting publicly.

3. **Redefine failure.** Early online silence is not humiliation. It is the learning stage, just like broken threads in weaving.

4. **Reframe visibility.** Showing your work online is no different from displaying your best piece in the mandi.

5. **Competitors will copy anyway.** Online, you gain timestamp proof that protects originality.

Reflection

Rafiq's hesitation was not about technology. It was about dignity. He feared laughter, gossip, and the weight of failure. His father's resistance was not a result of ignorance. It was a memory of how respect was earned slowly through tradition. Both needed to be reminded that they had changed before and survived.

The real breakthrough came not through argument but through evidence. A single photo on WhatsApp generated an immediate order. That order said what words could not. For the father, it proved online was not empty. For the son, it gave courage to try again.

Change often feels like a betrayal of tradition, but in reality, it is another chapter in the same story of survival. What worked yesterday will not always work tomorrow. To protect heritage, we must allow it to evolve.

Chapter 6: The Cost of Disconnection

**"The web does not just connect machines, it connects people.
And that's where trust has to live."**

- *Tim Berners-Lee*

The sprawling fields of Chhattisgarh, a mosaic of green and gold, told a story of hard work and a hopeful harvest. But for Suman Devi, the leader of the Kisan Kalyan Farmer Producer Organisation (FPO), it was a story with an unhappy conclusion. Her FPO, a collective of over 500 small farmers, grew some of the finest organic rice in the region. Their fields, nurtured without chemicals, produced a premium crop. They had embraced the digital world with enthusiasm, creating a detailed profile on the Farmer Connect platform and meticulously listing their "sell offers" on e-NAM, the national agricultural marketplace. They had done everything right, investing time and a small amount of capital in their digital presence. But the promise of better income remained elusive, and the frustration was a palpable weight in the modest office of their FPO.

I sat with her late one evening, the only light coming from the laptop screen illuminating her face. She scrolled through a list of transactions with a tired sigh. "The platforms are there, but the buyers are not," she told me, her voice a mix of quiet determination and weary disappointment. "Or they are, but they want to pay the same price as the middlemen. We spend hours listing our produce, taking photos, and managing our profile. But when an exporter calls, they ask for a lower price. The buyers don't know us. They don't trust our quality." For them, the FPO was just another listing, another number in a crowded digital marketplace.

Her frustration was a direct reflection of the problems highlighted in a recent report she had read, which stated that FPOs face "limited impact in market linkages" and are often burdened by "thin margins." The digital platforms had created a marketplace, but they hadn't built a community of trust. They had made a connection, but they hadn't established a relationship. Suman Devi recalled how the old middlemen, despite their flaws, offered something the digital world lacked: a handshake, a line of credit, and a reputation built on years of personal interaction. This was the social capital that was missing. The digital systems had removed the intermediary, but they had also removed the trust, forcing FPOs to compete on a soulless platform where price was the only factor.

The Buyer's Dilemma: Trusting the Unknown

Miles away, in a sleek corporate office in a bustling city, Mr. Jatin Shah, a mid-sized rice exporter, faced his own digital dilemma. He was a savvy businessman who wanted to source directly from FPOs to cut costs and create a more sustainable supply chain. He saw the potential for a win-win, but he was hesitant to risk his business on an unknown entity.

"I have a large contract on the table with a premium food distributor in Dubai. The client wants containers of consistently high-quality, organic rice. They need end-to-end traceability," he said, gesturing at a large-screen television where he was on a video call with his European client. "I see the FPOs on these portals, but how do I know if they are reliable? How do I know their quality is consistent? The data is so fragmented," he said, scrolling through a cluttered interface filled with low-resolution photos and incomplete product descriptions. "One FPO lists a low price, but what are their quality standards? Another FPO lists a high price, but they have no transaction history. The platform gives me a list, but it doesn't give me the most important thing: trust."

His frustration was palpable. He was about to give the large, profitable contract to a well-known aggregator, a large-scale intermediary who could guarantee the quality and consistency, but who would also take a significant cut. The disparity, as the report mentioned, was that the platforms were not "fully reaching the broader agricultural economy" because they lacked the fundamental element of a transparent, trusted history. Mr. Shah's dilemma was a perfect mirror of Suman Devi's. She had the product, he had the market, but the digital tools designed to connect them were failing to bridge the trust gap. The disconnection was costing them both.

The New Outlook: A Digital Ledger of Trust

The solution wasn't to build another platform. The platforms already existed, but they were transactional and commodity-focused. The solution was to build on top of an intelligent, distributed digital layer that would integrate with the existing ecosystem, directly addressing the core issues of trust and transparency. This decentralised digital layer, Blockchain, was not a brand-new, expensive piece of software. It was a digital protocol designed to build relationships by making trust a visible, data-backed asset.

This protocol was a simple, accessible module within the existing platforms. It didn't require new apps or expensive hardware. It was a digital system of verified transactions that created a public, transparent history for both buyers and sellers, which parties can verify.

1. Verified Transaction History: When Mr. Shah and Suman Devi decided to do a pilot deal, their transaction was logged on a private, shared digital ledger. This blockchain ledger recorded not just the transaction, but also the quality metrics

(verified by a third-party inspection upon delivery), the payment date and amount, and a rating from both parties on the transaction's success. This created a digital footprint of their relationship, an immutable record of their reliability.

2. Tiered Verification and Incentives: Over time, as Suman Devi's FPO completed more successful transactions verified by the system, her profile on the platform would be upgraded. A new module would display her FPO's "Trust Score", a rating based on its history of quality and timely deliveries. Additionally, it created a unique digital identity that can be integrated into other systems for identification purposes without requiring the sharing of personal credentials. This score, along with the unique digital identity, would be prominently displayed, providing a visual, data-backed signal to other buyers, such as Mr. Shah, that her FPO was a reliable partner. Similarly, Mr. Shah's profile would get a "Trusted Buyer" status based on his record of prompt payments. This system directly addressed the "lack of social capital" by building it digitally, rewarding consistent, trustworthy behaviour. The more they transacted transparently, the more valuable their digital reputation became.

3. Direct Incentive Protocol: The system also integrated a dynamic pricing model. Mr. Shah, wanting to encourage high quality and loyalty, could make an offer with a quality premium. If Suman Devi's FPO consistently delivered grains that met or exceeded the agreed-upon standards, the system would automatically add a bonus to her payment. This created a powerful, data-driven incentive that rewarded quality and consistency directly, bypassing the middlemen and their thin margins. This wasn't a one-time reward; it was a transparent system that encouraged long-term quality improvement.

The Return: From Fragmentation to a Partnership

The pilot project transformed their relationship. The Blockchain smart contract protocol did what the basic platforms couldn't. It built a bridge of trust. Mr. Shah received his order with a full, verifiable digital history of the grain's journey. The German client was so impressed by the level of traceability that they increased their next order. The trust he now had in Suman Devi's FPO was worth more than any price discount an aggregator could offer.

- For Suman Devi and her FPO: The ROI was in fair pricing and empowerment. The FPO was no longer competing on the lowest price. Their track record of quality and reliability, now visible to the world, earned them a premium. The blockchain-based smart contract ensured that payments were made on time, eliminating the uncertainty that had always plagued them. The FPO's digital reputation became an asset, attracting other buyers who were looking for reliable partners. They moved from being just another listing to a strategic supplier in a global value chain.

- For Mr. Jatin Shah: The ROI was in risk reduction and market access. He could now source from FPOs with confidence, knowing their history and quality were digitally verifiable. The new protocol gave him the transparency he needed to fulfil his international contracts. The direct relationship with Suman Devi's FPO meant he could secure a consistent, high-quality supply without paying a middleman's commission. He had found a way to support local farmers and improve his own bottom line, all by leveraging digital trust.

The story of Kisan Kalyan FPO became a success story on the platform, and other FPOs began to follow their lead. The digital system not only facilitated transactions but also created an environment of collaboration and shared success. The cost of

44

disconnection, as well as the frustration of both seller and buyer, was replaced by the value of a digital relationship built on data, transparency, and trust.

Mini-Framework: Building Digital Relationships

- Identify the Human Problem: The biggest barrier to digital transformation is often not technology, but a lack of trust and social capital. Identify these human problems first.

- Build on Existing Foundations: Avoid creating entirely new, expensive systems. Instead, build intelligent digital layers that add value to existing platforms and solve specific problems. Many companies operate in this domain, and skilled consultants are available for planning and implementation; consider seeking their expertise.

- Make Trust Tangible: Use digital tools to create a verifiable history of transactions, quality, and reliability. This makes trust a tangible, measurable asset.

- Incentivise Behaviour: Use digital systems to directly reward desired behaviour, like consistent quality and prompt payments. This creates a virtuous cycle of positive behaviour and shared success.

Reflection

The story of Suman Devi and Mr. Jatin Shah is a powerful reminder that digital transformation in the MSME and FPO space is not just about adopting technology; it's about building a better ecosystem. The existing platforms were a good start, but they were transactional in nature. They lacked the human elements of trust and relationships. By creating a digital protocol that captured these elements, both sides were able to unlock new value. The digital solution didn't just connect them; it gave them a reason to trust each other.

This transformation proved that the FPO model could be scaled and made more viable, not by creating a new marketplace, but by creating a digital layer that addressed the fundamental challenges of thin margins, trust, and market linkages. The digital tool became a way to build social capital, proving that technology can indeed be a powerful tool for empowerment, not just for a select few, but for every link in the value chain.

Chapter 7: The Culture Eats Digital Strategy Too

"Trust is built when transparency is paired with purpose."

— Adapted from Simon Sinek

It was a warm afternoon when I reached the Gokul Industrial Estate in Belgaum, Karnataka. The smell of metal filings and oil hung in the air as I walked past a row of machining units, each humming with life. These were businesses built on decades of craft, grit, and habit. I was here to meet the leadership of Rao Precision Cast, a small but growing second-generation enterprise that made components for pump and valve manufacturers across South India.

In the front office, I met Ms. Shalini Rao, the company's Managing Partner. Clad in a blue cotton kurta and sneakers, she exuded ease and quiet command. She was joined by her cousin and co-director, Arvind Rao, who handled production and procurement. As we settled into a sunlit conference room, I asked them what they felt when people spoke about digital tools like ERP or dashboards.

Shalini didn't hesitate. "We want to modernise, yes. But the moment someone says 'transparency', I see discomfort in the team. They think it means blame, not clarity."

Arvind added, "We've had foremen who've been here longer than I have. They know every sound a lathe makes. But if suddenly we show their numbers on a screen, it feels like an audit, not appreciation."

Additionally, a few employees resist digital transformation because they feel their activities are under constant scrutiny and may be analysed later. Everyone, at times, becomes a bit relaxed at work, not every day and not every hour; people are energetic and can deliver the same results, and that's okay. Additionally, we have observed that many employees become quite happy when digital systems break down or don't work efficiently. If you look into their eyes, they will be telling, "I told you, this digital doesn't work, trust in human beings." And next time, their natural reaction is, we saw what happened last time.

These weren't resistance. It was a legacy of resistance to anything new, fueled by a fear of being misunderstood and labelled as inefficient or questioned for their dedication and loyalty.

The Fear Beneath the Fear

This hesitation wasn't unique. In Ludhiana, a bicycle parts manufacturer once told me, "The day we put up the dashboard, my senior operator stopped talking to me for a week. He thought we were trying to catch him slipping."

And in Morbi, Gujarat, at a ceramic unit, a shift supervisor refused to use barcode tracking. "We've been meeting targets for years," he said. "Now you want a code to tell you what I did?"

What they feared wasn't the tool. It was the shift in perception that might trigger it.

I asked Shalini and Arvind what outcome they wanted.

"Better planning," she said. "Less fire-fighting. But not if it means we lose trust in our people."

A Gentle Start: Co-Create, Don't Impose

I told them about a food processing unit I had worked with near Madurai. The owner, a third-generation entrepreneur, had faced pushback when he announced digital logging of batch times and QC entries.

So instead of pushing a system, he sat down with his line supervisors and asked, "What slows you down every day?" They listed five recurring issues. Over the next month, they worked together to solve two of them using digital checklists that the team had designed themselves. The screens stayed in the factory, not the office.

By the time a dashboard was introduced, the data felt like their own. It wasn't a report card. It was a tool.

Back in Belgaum, Arvind leaned back, thinking. "If the team helps define what's tracked, they won't feel like it's being used against them."

Shalini smiled. "Let's try it. Start small. But start right." We will avoid words like "Tracking", Monitoring", etc and choose better, more inclusive words for these tools.

Tiny Trials, Big Shifts

The following week, they selected a single line for a pilot: tool life checking for two machines. No software, no new screens. Just a sheet on a clipboard near each station.

Operators noted when a tool started and when it was replaced. After two weeks, a pattern emerged: one tool brand lasted almost 20% longer than the others. This insight didn't spark blame. It sparked discussion.

In the next meeting, a senior machinist said, "If this saves money, we should try the same log for coolant usage." That moment changed everything.

The second pilot was downtime logging. But again, no names. Just causes. Air pressure drops. Late raw material. Minor alignment delays. In three weeks, the plant had cut reactive maintenance by 15%.

From Data to Dialogue, Not Drama. Nomenclature mattered.

They took inspiration from peers across India:

- A women-led packaging co-op in Jorhat, Assam, used colour-coded charts to highlight dispatch delays without naming departments.

- In Udaipur, a marble-cutting unit gamified safety audits; the shift with the fewest incidents got an extra tea break.

- In Goa, a bakery with just 12 staff created a wall chart that displayed order fulfilment timelines. It showed gaps, yes, but also celebrated consistency.

Transparency worked where trust was nurtured before numbers were shared. Words that evoked a feeling of being tracked and scrutinised were avoided and replaced with better words.

Reframing the Narrative

Shalini and Arvind gradually rolled out a digital dashboard, but only after three rounds of team feedback. What started with tool logs now includes on-time delivery stats, procurement delays, and power outages. Data was reviewed monthly in open circles, not closed cabins.

Three months in, their maintenance lead proposed reviewing energy usage by shift. "We'll know where the load spikes," he said. "It helps us all."

This wasn't top-down control. It was bottom-up insight.

Building Healthy Transparency

Fear	Reframe the Approach	Why It Works
It will trigger internal politics.	Co-design dashboards with team input	Reduces resistance and builds ownership
It will expose inefficiencies.	Focus on system gaps, not people's names, and avoid words that evoke the feeling of tracking, monitoring, etc	Keeps conversations constructive and removes the outright feeling of being tracked.
People will compete or blame.	Track team-level patterns, not individual performance	Promotes collaboration over comparison
Leadership will misuse insights.	Share goals and review findings together	Builds a culture of shared accountability

Reflection

Transparency doesn't cause politics. Ambiguity does. When teams co-own the systems that track their work, they feel valued, not watched. Shalini and Arvind didn't push for transformation. They invited it.

They didn't turn on a dashboard. They turned up the trust.

Chapter 8: Growth Without Losing The Reins

"Leadership is not about being in charge. It is about taking care of those in your charge."

– Simon Sinek

The tannery lanes of Kanpur carry their own music: the creak of pulley belts, the hiss of steam, and the smell of leather that lingers in the air. Inside one such workshop, Ramesh Bansal runs a modest leather goods unit with his wife and twenty workers. Wallets, belts, and keychains left his shop each week for local distributors.

Ramesh was a careful man. He kept every bill handwritten in bound registers, cross-checked payments personally, and even decided on the smallest purchases, such as thread. His staff respected him, but they also knew his style: nothing moved unless Ramesh approved it.

When we sat together in his office, he leaned across the desk and said what was on his mind.

"I want to expand. A large retailer has asked me to double the supply in six months. But tell me honestly, if I go digital, will I still be the one running my business, or will some system start running me?"

Fear of Losing the Grip

His wife, Sunita, walked in with two cups of tea and joined the conversation. "You know what worries him," she said. "Last year, we tried that accounting software. The consultant set it up, but only he knew the passwords. Every time we needed a report, we had to call him."

Ramesh nodded. "Exactly. I built this business with my hands. I cannot hand it over to a screen or an outsider."

Their supervisor, Imran, who had worked with them for ten years, added from the doorway, "Sir, even we feel helpless sometimes. When the consultant is unavailable. Workers stand waiting. We all feel tied."

The room fell quiet. The problem was not growth. The problem was the fear of losing command and not being in control of their own business.

The Tense Order

That afternoon, a large order came from a well-known export house. They wanted 5,000 leather belts, each with a different size mix, and delivery within three weeks. The old system of paper slips and verbal instructions began to crack.

On the second day, a mix-up happened. Two bundles of the wrong sizes reached the finishing line. Workers spent half a day correcting it, and Ramesh lost his temper. "This is what I mean," he said, throwing the slip on the desk. "If I don't check each step, the whole thing collapses."

Imran looked worried. "Sir, if we had a simple shared list, anyone could have seen the sizes before stitching. Right now, only you know everything."

Ramesh sighed. "But then how do I check and verify?"

Redefining Control

I picked up his register and said, "Right now, control means everything sits in your head and in your hand. But what if control could mean everyone sees the same truth at the same time? Then you are not losing power. You are spreading it."

Sunita leaned forward. "But spreading power is risky. What if they misuse it, and also, they are not that smart?"

I shook my head. "It is like driving a car. You do not control the engine by holding each piston. You control it with the steering wheel. Digital systems can become that steering wheel. You decide the direction, while others can run their part without waiting for you."

Ramesh listened. He did not argue.

Small Steps to Stay in Charge

We started by mapping what really mattered to him. He listed three key responsibilities: maintaining daily production numbers, keeping customer pricing confidential, and approving all payments.

"Then let us digitalise only these three first," I suggested. "No consultants holding passwords. The login remains with you. Others only update what they do."

Imran agreed to update a simple online file for daily production. Sunita volunteered to learn the digital payment system, but with Ramesh as the approver. A younger worker was assigned to scan and upload delivery challans so that Ramesh could review them at any time.

The systems were basic, but they kept Ramesh in the driver's seat.

The Same Export Order, Revisited

Two weeks later, the export house added a second order, this time for wallets. The shop was tense again, but this time the new method showed its strength.

Imran updated the production file daily. Workers could see the required sizes on a paper chart pinned to the wall or on a TV screen that Ramesh had installed on the production floor, allowing everyone to see what needed to be done. Sunita checked payments through the bank's online portal, but left final approval to Ramesh, who handled both the maker and checker processes. The scanned challans were neatly stored, and when the buyer called asking for proof, Ramesh pulled it up in seconds.

He smiled for the first time in days. "So the system is working for me, not over me."

Mini Framework: Mindset Shifts for Growth with Control

Step	Mindset Shift	Action to Take
1	Control does not mean secrecy	Share information but keep approval rights
2	Start small with core areas	Digitalise only the top 2–3 processes first
3	Keep ownership of access	Passwords and authorisations remain with leaders
4	Train trusted people	Build capacity within the family and staff

5	Use systems as steering wheels	Decide direction, let others run their part

Reflection

For Ramesh Ji, growth once felt like surrendering the business to outsiders. What he discovered was the opposite. By opening up a few processes while keeping the final keys in his hands, he gained more visibility, not less. His people worked with greater confidence, and his own stress levels were reduced. Control was no longer about checking every stitch but about ensuring the whole workshop moved in the same direction.

Chapter 9: Speed Without Losing Control

"Start where you are. Use what you have. Do what you can."

- **Arthur Ashe**

Itanagar wakes before the mist lifts from the hills. Outside Ganga Market, shutters rise, and the smell of steamed momos mixes with petrol from early scooters. On NH 415, a three-floor building carries a simple board in blue paint. Hillview Skills Centre. Inside, a courtyard holds two training bays for two-wheeler repair and basic electrical wiring. A classroom on the first floor teaches front office and housekeeping for hotels. A wooden noticeboard near the stairs shows fee dates and placement interviews written in chalk.

Teresa Koyu owns the centre. She started with four trainers and now employs twenty. About two hundred and fifty students pass through the rooms each year. Her operations head is Pema Thapa. Her senior electrical instructor is Nabam Takar. Cash fees are collected at a steel desk with a register that has grown wide with taped pages.

I asked Teresa what she thinks when people say digital first.

"Digital is for tech-savvy people in metros," she said. "We are a small town setup. I began with a noticeboard, a phone, and basic digital tools. I will not risk the centre on apps I do not understand."

Pema flipped open last month's fee register. Two receipts were missing signatures. One student had paid in two parts on different days and was marked only once. A placement partner from a hotel in Guwahati had called on Wednesday for twelve trainees. The call came when Teresa was at the workshop bay. By the time Pema returned the call, the hotel had closed with another institute that replied to the message with the quotation within ten minutes.

"That is the part that hurts," Teresa said. "I lost the hotel, not because my trainees are weak. I lost it because we moved slowly on the phone."

Nabam looked up from a bench with spare plugs and wires. "Our wiring classes run fine," he said. "We finish on time. But students stand in line on fee days, and the crowd wastes a good hour."

Teresa held her ground. "I am not ready for a system. If the net fails or some company changes plans, my records must still stand."

We agreed to a two-week trial that would not disturb the register. No new software purchases. No change to teaching hours. Only small steps that remove slow points.

A very small trial inside the current routine

Pema proposed three moves that felt like common sense.

First, fee collection with proof. The desk kept its cash box and register. In addition, a QR code was placed on the counter with a small sign. Pay here if you prefer. The receipt number was entered in the register as usual. Students who paid by scan received an auto message with their roll number and amount. Pema added a rule. If the net dropped, the cash and the register stayed in charge. No one was turned away.

Second, an inquiry form that never sleeps. A simple form link and a QR code were printed on one sheet and stuck on the board. It asked for name, phone, program, and preferred start month. Pema placed a small box below the board with the same four lines on paper for those who preferred a slip. Every evening, one trainee copied paper slips into the link. The centre kept its habit of callbacks. The link only held all names in one place.

Third, a placement broadcast list with two fixed windows. Pema created a broadcast list of companies that usually hire. At nine forty-five in the morning, he sent a single line with the current availability by trade and batch. At four fifteen, he sent a short update if counts changed; no group chat. Calls for details stayed on voice. The register noted each confirmed interview.

Teresa listened to the plan and nodded because none of it removed the register. Each step added speed but left control inside the room. Definitely, their tasks were going to increase as they had to match both digital and physical register details. What if one student does both? However, we needed to start with a demo to demonstrate ease and also how the customer's priorities and behaviour have shifted more towards digital.

What the first week showed

On Tuesday, the fee rush began at ten. Seventy students came to the desk throughout the day. About a third chose to scan. The queue moved faster because there was less money to count and give change back. Pema stapled the scan confirmation to the paper receipt for that roll number and wrote the receipt number in the register. At four, a parent arrived in a hurry and paid by scan. Teresa looked at the message on the phone and said, "Take the class. We will staple the slip at five." The parent smiled and left without delay.

On Wednesday, the hotel from Guwahati that had chosen another institute the previous week sent a new request for four front office trainees. Pema replied with the nine forty-five line that was already on schedule. Four available. Joining ready. Interview any day this

59

week. The response came back in one minute. Send tomorrow. The trainees left the next morning on the first bus.

On Thursday, a two-wheeler service centre owner from Naharlagun walked in with his nephew. He pointed to the inquiry print. "We filled this last night," he said. "Thank you for calling at ten sharp." Earlier, he would have waited for a missed call to be noticed. Now, Pema saw the form list at 9:30 and called in order. The room did not change its routine. The list changed the order of calls.

By Friday, Nabam asked for one more small step. He wanted to post next week's wiring practical slots without crowding the board. Pema added the timetable as a pinned message on the centre's number and as a print below the board. Students began to check the message before asking the desk.

The hesitation behind the hesitation

In week two, Teresa voiced a deeper worry. "If we put our counts on a broadcast, will other centres copy and flood the market?"

Pema answered from the desk. "The line is short by design. One sentence. It is enough for our partners to plan. Anyone else cannot use it without a history with us."

That afternoon, the power dropped in the lane for an hour. The QR code went idle. Fees continued in cash with the register. The day did not break.

At the end of the month, Teresa opened the register and read the notes with Pema. Fee days were calmer. The queue time was reduced, and fewer parents stood waiting. There were no missing signatures because scanned receipts brought a second proof to staple. Reconciliation at the end of the day was cleaner and took less time to complete.

Likewise, inquiry handling improved. The printed link and the paper slip box together created one clean list. Fewer names were lost to missed calls or scraps of paper. Pema stopped writing names on the back of fee receipts.

Placement calls were sharper. When the morning line went out, two employers replied within ten minutes. Interviews were fixed early in the day rather than late in the evening when trainers were on their way home. One dealer in Naharlagun requested three additional electrical trainees after reviewing the line for the second time. The centre did not create jobs. It reduced the distance between readiness and response.

No one bought software. The register stayed as the final book. The new steps were habits that did not ask the room to become something it was not.

Conversations that moved the room

A parent from Chimpu returned after paying by scan the previous week.

"This is easier," she said. "I can see the message at once. I still want a paper receipt for my file."

Teresa handed the paper and smiled. "You will always get paper," she said. "The message helps us both."

A young trainee asked if the centre would take classes on the phone. Nabam answered before Teresa could speak.

"We will practice with tools, not replace the bench," he said. "You will still wire a board with your hands. Digital will tell you your slot and your interview. The rest is work."

A hotel manager from Tezpur called to thank Pema for the morning line.

"When I see your one sentence," he said, "I plan my week. It saves me two trips."

What digital first meant here

Teresa wrote one rule on a paper and pinned it above the desk. Before we do a step manually, we will ask if there is a more straightforward digital way that fits our room and shows a return this month. If yes, we try. If not, we keep the manual step.

The rule kept the centre calm. Students paid, classes ran, and placements moved. The centre did not try to become an app. It attempted to ask the right first question.

Mini Framework: Digital first without losing the room

- Keep the register as the final book for the first month until you become comfortable with digital. Don't go all in one go. Scans and messages support it.

- Create one inquiry list that never sleeps. A simple link for those who can scan, and a paper slip box for those who prefer paper. Copy slips once a day.

- Send one message twice a day; one sentence at a fixed time. Calls stay on voice.

- Post messages in two places, as a pinned message in the online group and another on the physical board. Questions reduced, confusions resolved.

- Fix a boundary for silence. No groups. No long captions. No spamming.

- Keep track of what the digital is helping you with and how you can utilise the saved data for increased efficiency or revenue.

Reflection

The centre began with a belief that digital is for big cities and big minds. In practice, a digital-first mindset did not mean buying a system or running the centre on a screen. It meant asking one small question at the right moment. Can this step be done faster or safer on the phone without changing who we are? Fees moved with less friction. Inquiries were not lost. Placement calls became early and clear. The room kept its bench, its board, and its register. Control did not leave the desk. It became easier to see.

Section 2: The Cost & Trust Concerns

Even when the mindset starts to shift, the next big question is: *"But is it worth it?"* MSMEs often operate on razor-thin margins. The cost of digital adoption, the fear of audits, data privacy concerns, and the risk of hidden traps can feel overwhelming. This section addresses those fears head-on, showing how digital actually saves more than it costs, protects more than it exposes, and ultimately builds trust rather than breaking it.

Chapter 10: "Human staff are cheaper and better."

"Technology is best when it brings people together."
— *Matt Mullenweg (Co-founder, WordPress)*

The clock was a quarter past ten in Lucknow, and the sun was already blazing. I stood within the premises of Verma Book Depot, an old wholesale shop sandwiched between a peeling paint hardware store and a neon-lit mobile repair shop, and the bookstore seemed untouched by time.

The interior was dominated by floor-to-ceiling bookshelves creaking under the weight of textbooks, guides, notebooks, and registers. There was a worn-out wooden counter in the middle, behind which Mr. Rakesh Verma, the proprietor, was engrossed in overseeing three workers loading cartons.

He spotted me, inclined his head, and then resumed bellowing, "Check the SKU! Don't cross-pile the Class 10 and Class 12 stock!"

As the commotion subsided, we were finally able to converse.

"Everyone talks about digital, but we manage just fine with trusted people, and I feel it's economical too," he said.

He opened a thick ledger and flipped to the page for today's sales. The handwriting was tight, the columns crammed. "See, all this is manual. But it works. My staff understands it, and it's cheaper too."

Rakesh ji wasn't against digital out of fear; he simply didn't see the point.

"For a business like mine, human staff are faster. Why invest in something they already do?" he asked. "I've been running this way for 20 years."

There was no fear in his tone. Just familiarity. Habit. Stability. But as we spoke further, small cracks began to show.

I asked him if he had ever experienced stock mismatches, and he sighed.

"It does. Occasionally, a few extra books get sent out accidentally. Occasionally, returns do not arrive. Occasionally, an item is entered twice in two different locations. Little problems."

Little problems that silently eroded his margins.

I bent over and told him, "Rakesh ji, "Your staff are vital, no question. But only humans err. Tech enables us to learn from them."

He nodded, but with a shrug. "And you also have to understand the machinery, that takes time too".

"Absolutely", I said. "But even one staff member with a simple inventory app can tell you where things go wrong.

I took out my phone and opened a free demo of an inventory management application. "Suppose you get 500 Class 10 textbooks. The app records it. When a carton is shipped out, the change is reflected. If something is missing or duplicated, you'll be notified immediately. And when an employee quits, his information doesn't."

He observed as I added and subtracted items in real time. His expression changed from one of opposition to one of interest.

I reminded him that this wasn't about replacing his people, but about assisting them in working smarter, so that they feel less stressed, can work efficiently, and utilise the time to do something more for the business. Most small businesses begin with one employee using technology, then gradually increase their adoption of it. This will also help companies like his to view the information on the admin dashboard, allowing them to track stocks, types of errors, and more, so that they can address these issues and train their employees accordingly.

The Moment of Shift

He summoned his younger assistant, Rahul. "Look at this, do you understand it?

Rahul picked up the phone and began experimenting. In minutes, he learned to add products, input quantities, and view outgoing stock.

"I can try, sir," Rahul replied.

Rakesh ji glanced at me. "Let's experiment with this for a month. Let's see if it's any different."

I was curious to know, just as a movie climax, what happens after one month, would they uninstall the application? Rahul got fired as he may have made a mistake, or they are using the application regularly. Keeping my fingers crossed, I visited the shop, as I couldn't hold my excitement for longer than that, and I also didn't want to disturb them with the same pitch of digital repeatedly. I did my best and I was happy. But excitement was not getting settled.

67

This time, I thought I must buy a book, and I asked Rahul, 'Do you have this book?'

Oh, wow, he took out the mobile app, searched for the book's name, and told me, 'Yes, I will get it; it's in the third row, second shelf.' I was impressed by his memory and precision, as he made it look effortless. I said, "You have a great memory," and he replied, "Sir, it's your suggestion to use the stock inventory application that made this possible. Now, the errors are fewer, and Sir is also happy. We can now sell online as well, since we have a digital stock of all the books".

What a progress and relief! Rahul's confidence, along with a separate marked section in the shop for e-commerce dispatch, explained it all.

It wasn't a dramatic change. But it was a telling change, from assumption to experiment.

Digital doesn't replace human hands; it holds them steady.

While reflecting on the entire situation, I realised that no one external can push for and implement the required change; there has to be one or a few tech champions in each organisation who can drive the change. It just needs a nudge and a deep understanding of the pain point. This was a classic case. I have seen many people uninstall the application after a few hours or days, not because they don't understand it, but because there is no owner buy-in or an internal tech champion pushing the case too strongly. So, I scribbled the following on a piece of paper.

The "One-Person Digital Pilot".

Purpose: De-risk digital adoption by using the most tech-savvy staff member, whom the owner or seniors can rely on and who faces the frequent challenges related to the pain point.

Pilot Phase	Who tries it	Digital Load	Duration	Expected outcome
Seed	Tech-curious junior staff	Low (1-2 tasks per day)	2-4 weeks	Ease of use, build confidence
Expand	Trusted senior/owner's kin	Medium (core tasks)	1-3 months	Partial adoption, contextual adjustments
Embed	Internal/external champion	High (full integration)	3-12 months	ROI visibility, business transformation

Chapter 11: The Cost of Convenience

"Beware of little expenses; a small leak will sink a great ship."

— Benjamin Franklin

Two knitting machines filled most of the room, their belts running with a steady clatter. Bundles of wool lay in blue crates near the doorway. Kamaljit Singh stood with a grease rag in one hand and a slip of paper in the other. His wife, Jaspreet, sat on a charpai near the counter, folding finished pairs of socks and tying them in dozens with red thread. Their son, Lakhvinder, had just come in from college and was wiping dust off a small desktop that looked older than him.

Kamaljit spoke first. "Let me say it straight. My buyers pay in cash. I like it. I can pay the yarn man, I can pay workers, and I can keep the place moving. If I depend on online money, I will wait for messages, stand in lines, and lose half a day."

He was not angry. He sounded tired. The machines hummed behind him like a reminder of the day's targets.

I asked what troubled him most. He tapped the slip. "The yarn man has new stock today. He wants cash by evening. If I tell him I will transfer online, he will say Send someone to the shop with cash. How do I run a room like this without cash in my pocket?"

Jaspreet looked up. "Saturday is wage day. Our people do not want explanations. They want money on time. If even one week is late, the whole lane will talk."

Lakhvinder leaned on the counter. "Papai, not everything has to be cash. We can keep cash for wages and small buys, and still take big payments online."

Kamaljit shook his head. "This is a room, not a lecture hall. If buyers send money late, nothing runs."

The call from Delhi

The landline rang. Jaspreet picked up the receiver and handed it to Kamaljit. "It is Madam Ritu from Delhi."

He put the phone on speaker. A clear voice filled the room. "Kamaljit ji, I need four thousand pairs in white, mixed sizes, delivery in three days. I can confirm the order today."

Kamaljit smiled at the ceiling fan. "Done, Madam. Send the cash advance with the truck driver like last time."

There was a pause on the other end. "No driver this time. We will arrange transport. I will transfer the advance as soon as you send me a digital invoice. I want confirmation before five in the evening."

Kamaljit covered the mouthpiece with his hand and looked at me. "You see the problem."

Sameer spoke softly. "Madam, we will send the invoice in an hour."

After the call ended, Kamaljit turned to him. "Invoice in an hour on what. What if the money comes at night? The yarn man will not wait."

Lakhvinder did not react. "If we can send the invoice quickly, the money can come quickly. Let me try."

71

Where cash looked strong and where it was weak

While Lakhvinder sat at the old desktop and opened a blank document, I asked Kamaljit to walk me through the real costs of his cash routine.

"How many times do you visit the yarn dealer and the bank in a week?"

"Two or three times."

"How long does it take each time?"

"An hour, sometimes more."

"So, five or six hours a week," I said. "During busy weeks, even more. At your machine rate, those hours could produce fifty more pairs. That is about five thousand in value."

He stared at the floor. Jaspreet added quietly, "And do not forget the week you lost twenty thousand near the mandi. And the fake notes last winter."

Kamaljit did not argue. "Cash has risks. I know. But online makes me wait."

"Waiting is a cost only if the rest of the system stands still," I said. "If big payments come online, you can pay the yarn man from the account on the same day. You do not need to withdraw everything."

He folded the slip in his hand until it became a tight square. "What if the yarn man refuses?"

"Then link speed to his interest," I said. "Tell him payments from the account will reach him the same day, and that you will pay a small advance now and the balance by evening once Delhi confirms. People move when their benefit is clear."

A new problem appears

Pritam, the senior worker, hurried in from the lane. "Sahab, the transport man says the road near the bypass is jammed. If the order does not leave tomorrow morning, it will arrive late in Delhi."

Kamaljit rubbed his forehead. "If I miss this, I will look unreliable. Madam will reduce orders next month."

Sameer lifted his head from the keyboard. "All the more reason to move fast. If we share the invoice now, Madam can proceed with the transfer. We can pay the yarn man at four, cut and stitch tonight, pack by morning, and load before the jam becomes worse."

Kamaljit looked at me. "What if the transfer comes late?"

"Call her, confirm the bank name and the mode. Share the account details properly on the invoice. Ask her to send the reference number by message. You will see it on your phone even before the bank SMS."

He did not love the plan, but he picked up the phone.

Negotiation with the yarn dealer

While Lakhvinder created the invoice, Kamaljit dialled Mr Nanda, the yarn dealer. "Nanda ji, I will bring five thousand in cash now. I will pay the balance online by evening as soon as a transfer arrives from Delhi. I will send you a screenshot. You will have your full payment today."

There was a long silence. Then Nanda said, "If you send me a photo of the transfer, I will release the full lot. Do not come twice. I will keep a boy ready at the shutter."

Kamaljit exhaled. "Done."

He put down the phone and looked at Jaspreet. "This will work only if the money comes fast."

Lakhvinder printed the invoice, checked a few numbers with his mother, took a photo on his phone, and sent it to Ritu Madam with a short message. "Invoice attached. Please confirm the advance transfer. We will share dispatch details at night."

The four hours that changed the room

At two thirty, no message. At three, no message. The room felt heavy. Workers whispered near the machine. Pritam kept checking the clock.

At three ten, Sameer's phone buzzed. "Madam has asked for our GST number on the invoice header."

Jaspreet frowned. "We forgot to add it."

Lakhvinder updated the file, printed again, took a photo, and sent it within ten minutes.

At three forty, a new message arrived. "Transfer initiated. Reference number is in the message."

Sameer read the number aloud. Kamaljit opened his banking app. The balance was still unchanged. He stared at the screen as if it would move faster under pressure. At three fifty-two, the number on the screen jumped. He did not speak. He held the phone out for the others to see. Jaspreet smiled. Pritam slapped his palm gently and hurried to the back to start cutting.

Kamaljit called Nanda. "The amount has reached. Look at the screenshot." Nanda replied, "Take the lot now. I will keep the shutter half open. Send your boy."

Work that felt lighter

The room shifted shape after that. Two workers began packing. Lakhvinder arranged sizes on a whiteboard so that no bundle would go missing. Jaspreet labelled cartons with a thick marker. Pritam checked the stitching count against the list every hour. By nine at night, twenty cartons stood by the door. The truck man sent a photo of the loading time he had reserved for them near dawn. When I left, the radio was still on, and nobody looked tired anymore.

In the morning, Lakhvinder sent the dispatch photo and the challan to Ritu Madam. Her reply came before breakfast. "Good, keep this format. Next month, I will send a larger order."

Kamaljit looked at the phone and then at his wife. "I never thought speed would come from a screen," he said. "I thought speed only comes from cash in a pocket."

Jaspreet said what nobody else had said aloud. "Speed also comes from not running to the bank three times."

What the numbers said one week later

Lakhvinder made a small sheet of paper.

- Two large buyers paid online, which meant no counting of cash at night and no risk of fake notes.

- Payments to the yarn dealer shifted from three trips a week to one, as they now paid from the account for the larger quantities.

- Withdrawals for wages now happened once a week, not every other day.

- Machine time recovered from bank trips added up to almost five hours, which meant about fifty extra pairs in a busy week.

Kamaljit read the list and tapped the last line. "This is the only line that pays for everything else."

He kept cash for transactions that required immediate hand-to-hand settlement and used digital transactions for those that needed proof, speed, and scale. The room had not become a different room. It had become a calmer one.

Mini framework: when cash, when digital

Use cash for:

- Daily wages where workers prefer hand payment, and it's urgent, non-negotiable

- Small, urgent market purchases where the seller does not accept transfer

- Very minor repairs or tips that keep the day moving

Use digital for:

- Big buyer payments, so there is a record and faster reconciliation

- Supplier settlements, where a transfer and a screenshot can release material sooner

- Building a clean history with the bank and the accountant

- Reducing the number of bank visits, which returns machine time to production

Guardrails to keep control:

- Keep a small float in cash for two days of routine needs

- Keep a working balance in the account for supplier payments and emergencies

- Check the account on the phone twice a day, morning and evening

- Do one withdrawal a week for wages, not many small ones

- Write a simple rule on a paper near the counter that says who pays what, in cash or digital, so the team never guesses

Reflection

Kamaljit always believed cash was control. He liked the weight of it in his hand and the speed with which it solved a problem in the lane. What he learned in one tense afternoon was that speed comes from clarity more than it comes from currency. When a buyer pays on time and a supplier releases stock on the same day, and when a worker sees wages arrive without drama, the room breathes easier. Cash still lives in the drawer, but it no longer decides the day. The work does.

Chapter 12: The ROI of Digital Operations

"The biggest challenge in business is not competition, it is complacency."

-   Azim Premji

The industrial estate of Barasat, West Bengal, hummed with the deep, throaty thrum of machinery. Inside Allied Chemicals & Dyes, a medium-sized manufacturer of industrial pigments and dyes, the air was a complex mosaic of scents: the sharp tang of solvents, the earthy aroma of fine powders, and the faint, metallic smell of heated vats. This was a business built on tangible reality. Its value was measured in the weight of a finished drum and the clarity of a newly mixed pigment. The managing director, Arjun Sen, was a man of detail, his hands stained with years of working on the floor. His mind, however, was a running tally of batch numbers, production cycles, and market prices. His focus was on output; he was sceptical of anything that did not directly contribute to more product leaving the door.

I sat with him and the Head of Production, Mr. Khanna, in a small, glass-walled office that overlooked the factory floor. The day's production schedule, a large whiteboard filled with handwritten notes and erasures, was a testament to their established processes. It was a system that relied on experience and tribal knowledge.

"I know what you're here for," Arjun began, gesturing to a stack of paper invoices. "We have an ERP system for finance, and our marketing is on LinkedIn. But production is a living, breathing thing. We track every batch manually. We have supervisors on the floor who know the viscosity by sight and a pigment's shade by feel. They are our real sensors. What's the ROI of putting a digital sensor on a vat? Will it make the chemicals any better? My primary concern isn't about saving a few minutes. It's about a new system crashing, and a hundred people standing idle. What's the return on that kind of risk?"

Mr. Khanna, a veteran of the factory floor, nodded in solemn agreement. "We have our rhythms. The real cost is in a line stoppage, not in a missing signature. A digital breakdown could cost us a full day's production."

Their apprehension was clear and deeply rooted. They weren't against technology in principle; they were afraid of replacing a system of human experience and trust with one of abstract data and potential failure. Their focus was on the immediate, visible cost of a possible disruption, not the unseen costs of their current inefficiencies: the hidden leaks of time and money that were costing them a fortune.

The problem came into sharp focus just a few weeks prior. An urgent order from a major client required a specific shade of blue dye. The order was processed, the raw materials were procured, and the production team began mixing. However, a junior supervisor had misread a handwritten note on the batch sheet. He added a few extra kilos of a costly base chemical, a mistake that went unnoticed. By the time the final quality check was done, the batch was an off-shade, unsalvageable. The client, angry at the delay, threatened to cancel the contract. The lost revenue, the cost of the wasted materials, and the sheer chaos of a frantic rework day highlighted the vulnerability of their entire manual process. It was a crisis that nearly brought the business to its knees.

The Three-Point Pilot Project: A Strategic Investment

I proposed a small-scale pilot project for their most complex product line, the high-grade industrial dyes. The project focused on three key areas where their human-driven processes were most prone to error, delay, and financial loss. The goal was to prove, with data, that the ROI was in avoiding these hidden costs.

1. IoT-Enabled Production Vats: We installed simple, affordable Internet of Things (IoT) sensors on a few vats. These sensors were not meant to control the machines; they were digital observers. They monitored the temperature and viscosity in real-time, streaming the data to a shared dashboard. The workers still ran the mixers by hand, but the dashboard provided an objective, constant log. It was a digital helper, a tireless assistant that never blinked, never grew tired, and never misread a note. It captured every data point, giving them an auditable trail of the entire mixing process. The cost was minimal, amounting to less than a single batch's worth of raw materials.

2. Digital Batch Management: We replaced handwritten batch logs with a simple, tablet-based application. The old process involved a carbon copy book where a supervisor would write down every ingredient, its weight, and the time it was added. These books were prone to smudges, misreadings, and, often, being misplaced entirely. The new process was intuitive. When a worker added a new ingredient, they would simply scan a QR code on the raw material drum. This action automatically updated the digital batch record with the exact quantity, time, and the worker's ID. This created a traceable, auditable trail for every batch, from its first ingredient to its final drum.

3. Cross-Departmental Dashboards: The data from the production floor was no longer trapped on a whiteboard or in a paper log. It was automatically fed into a central system with custom-built dashboards for each department head. Ms. Sharma, the Head of Sales, could now see the real-time production status of an order and accurately promise a delivery date to clients without ever having to call the floor. Mr. Iyer, the Head of Finance, could view the raw material consumption and track the exact cost per batch, giving him a level of granular insight he had never had before. This single point of truth reduced friction and eliminated the need for manual reporting and inter-departmental inquiries.

The pilot ran for one quarter. The only cost was the sensors and a subscription to the cloud software. The company's existing network and internet were sufficient. The factory floor's rhythm did not change, but the information flow did. The ROI, as Arjun would soon discover, was in the quiet prevention of disaster.

The Return: From Hidden Costs to Measurable Value

The results of the pilot were not in a new sales contract but in a quantifiable reduction of invisible costs. The returns were not just about money; they were about peace of mind and the ability to grow.

- Waste Reduction: The IoT sensors detected a subtle temperature fluctuation in one of the vats that a supervisor, relying on human perception, might have missed. The dashboard flashed a warning. By correcting the temperature in real-time, they prevented an entire batch of dye from being wasted, saving over ₹ 75,000 in materials alone. Before, such losses were written off as "human error" and factored into the cost of doing business. Now, the data provided a clear reason and a tangible solution.

- Reduced Rework: In the past, about 3% of their batches required rework due to minor quality variations or mixing errors. During the pilot, the digital batch log caught an incorrect quantity of a costly pigment before it was added to the mixture. A senior worker, used to the old routine, had reached for the wrong drum. The tablet's alert prevented the mistake, saving a full day of rework and labour. This single instance of prevention was a powerful demonstration of the system's value.

- Improved On-Time Delivery: The sales team's new ability to track production progress in real-time meant they no longer had to make guesswork-based promises to clients. On one occasion, a major client's order was running slightly behind schedule. The Head of Sales, instead of making an excuse, called the client with a confident new date. "The system shows your batch is in the final stages of a quality check, and will be on the truck by tomorrow morning," she explained. The client, impressed by the precision, said, "That level of detail is a first for us. We appreciate the transparency." Their on-time delivery rate for that product line went from 88% to 96%.

- Faster Dispute Resolution: A key client in Hyderabad called to complain about a colour mismatch. In the past, this would have involved a full-scale audit, pulling paper records from a dusty cabinet, and a potential debit note. This time, Arjun's team could pull up the exact batch number, show the digital logs for raw materials, and confirm the precise shade code was used. The data proved their process was sound. The dispute was resolved in a single, five-minute call. The proof had travelled faster than the doubt, and the client, instead of issuing a debit note, placed a new, larger order.

At the end of the quarter, Arjun looked at the comprehensive ROI report. "I was worried about systems running the business," he said, tapping a finger on a line showing a 25% reduction in production waste. "What I found is that systems can make the business run smoothly. The real ROI wasn't in new sales. It was in avoiding the costs of our old, non-digital processes. This is not a luxury; it's a necessity for growth."

Mini-Framework: The ROI Equation for a Larger Business

- Identify the Hidden Costs: For a medium to large business, the most significant ROI is in addressing problems that are not obvious on the balance sheet: rework, line stoppages, and departmental friction. The cost of a few hours of manual work is nothing compared to the price of a misplaced order or a dissatisfied client.

- Focus on Process, Not Just Profit: Digital transformation at this scale is about building scalable, traceable, and repeatable processes. The financial return is a natural byproduct of that efficiency. It's about moving from a reactive to a proactive model.

- Use Data to Empower, Not to Control: The goal of digital tools is to give your team better, real-time information to make faster, more accurate decisions. The data should guide, not replace, human expertise.

- Pilot, Don't Overhaul: The fear of a large-scale system failure is real and valid. Start with a specific, high-risk product line or a single department. Prove the value of the digital solution before you scale it to the entire organisation.

Reflection

Arjun Sen's initial apprehension was a valid one for any medium-sized business. The fear of disruption, of losing control, and of a system failing is a powerful deterrent to change. But what he discovered was that his old system, reliant on memory, paper, and manual logs, was already failing him in subtle, expensive ways. He was losing money and time in the quiet spaces between departments, in the minor errors that cascaded into large ones.

The shift to a digital-first approach for his core operations wasn't about adding a new layer of complexity. It was about creating a single, transparent, and immutable source of truth that every department could rely on. It didn't replace his people; it made them more effective. The ROI wasn't a sudden, visible profit but a sustained reduction in the costs of friction, waste, and human error. He learned that the most significant ROI of a digital system is the confidence it gives you to make a better decision, every time.

Chapter 13: The Cost of the Paper Trail

"What got you here won't take you there."

- Marshall Goldsmith

The landscape of Hyderabad was a symphony of creation. Tower cranes moved like patient arms above green safety nets. Mixers turned from sunrise to nightfall. Near Gachibowli, a plain board read VK Urban Projects. Inside, a planning table held drawings of four live sites, a conference room had a wall screen, and a steel almirah guarded the finance room. The almirah held ledgers that only Vinod Reddy had access to. Vinod had grown from petty contracts to mid-sized and now large turnkey work. He still trusted the methods that felt safe to him: cash for wages, paper slips, and deals sealed with a voice and memory.

I met him at a high-rise site where rebar cages lay ready for lifts. He counted wage packets with the site cashier as a long queue edged forward in the shade. "My business breathes because it bends," he said, watching the roll call. "If I put every rupee on a screen, ten departments will arrive with files. I am not hiding; I pay taxes honestly. I am just avoiding noise."

His son, Ravi, joined us with a yellow hard hat and a tablet. He managed vendor coordination and progress updates. He knew his father's fear, and he also knew what that fear was costing them.

Back at the office, a bank letter lay on the conference table. The bank had declined an increase to their working capital limit, citing a lack of verifiable, system-generated project statements and timely statutory filings. The next file was a public works tender for a sports complex in Uppal, which required a digital audit trail, electronic invoicing, stage-linked payments, and fortnightly progress evidence. Vinod closed both files and reached for the almirah keys.

After our lengthy discussion and the push from Ravi, Vinod agreed to take the help of a consultant, so he called the chartered accountant, Clara D'Souza, who had guided several construction firms through scale without drama. She came the next morning, opened a notebook, and listened.

"What do you fear most?" she asked. "What must not break this month? What do you want in the next year?"

Vinod replied in order. "I fear long visits from officers. I will not disturb wage days. I want to win one large tender without begging suppliers for extended credit."

Clara drew a short plan that respected those lines. She proposed a single clean lane that could carry both compliance and speed. It would begin on a new site and would not touch other sites until it proved itself. It would make audits predictable rather than painful. It would keep control in the office, not in a vendor's server.

Part One: Basic Discipline That Paid from Day One

Clara introduced five habits.

1. A sweep and float rule: Each site kept a fixed two-day cash float. All extra collections and advances are swept into the bank every third evening. This lowered idle cash and built a bank trail without choking the site.
2. A receipt mirror: Sites continued to give paper slips. Every slip was photographed into a private office thread and

exported as a single PDF at the end of the day. The paper and the image sat together. The trail doubled without cost.

3. A clean room device: One phone per site was used only for banking, filings, and official documents. It lived in a drawer. Access sat with Ravi, supported by Clara. When proof was requested, they knew where to look.

4. A vendor ladder: Suppliers were tagged as A, B, or C. A meant electronic invoice and bank payment. B meant invoice with GST and occasional cash adjustments. C meant hand slips. Every fortnight, one C moved to B or one B moved to A by linking faster payment to clean documents.

5. A three-tick Friday ritual: Cash, bank, and day sheets were matched every Friday at six. Only when all three agreed did the page get three ticks. Gaps were closed the same day.

Vinod agreed because none of this handed away control. It simply made his room easier to defend. He was also happy to see his son working harder and trying to bring the change he wanted him to, so that he could gradually hand over the reins to him.

Part Two: High-End Tools That a Medium Firm Can Justify

Ravi brought the second set with clear business goals and took the help of another sharp technology consultant, Sudhir, focusing on faster payments, lower rework, cleaner vendor control, and fewer disputes.

1. A 4D Building Information Model: For each new project, the model tied the planned schedule to the building's shape across time. The team could see the planned slab pour on the screen for the coming week, bringing clarity to sequencing and vendor calls.

2. A digital twin: The twin sat on a secure cloud folder, showing the current state of the building against the plan. It pulled in three feeds: weekly drone maps for progress, logs from concrete maturity sensors, and gate logs from material

scanning. The twin allowed the project manager to check whether a stage met the release condition without waiting for fifteen phone calls.

3. Concrete maturity sensors: Small, disposable sensors were placed in the pour. They logged temperature and time and produced a simple strength estimate. The engineer could accept a shutter removal based on the logged curve, saving two wasted days and reducing rework.

4. Weekly drone flights: A licensed operator flew a fixed grid and produced progress maps and volume estimates for stockpiles. The maps were timestamped and stored in the month pack.

5. RFID and QR tagging at the gate: Steel bundles and cement pallets received tags upon arrival. The gate scanner produced an auto-generated receipt and pushed counts to the site store list. Losses from wrong counts or duplicate slips dropped.

6. Smart contract escrow for stage payments: On select private projects, a neutral wallet released payment when three proofs were uploaded for a stage: the twin snapshot, the engineer sign-off, and the gate receipt reconciliation. Payment delays were reduced, and both sides felt protected.

7. Electronic invoicing: Site bills were routed to finance through a simple workflow and assigned a serial number, which the bank also received. Reconciliation time got reduced.

8. A software bot in finance: The bot picked vendor invoices, read key fields, and filled the draft entry in the accounting system. A human checked and posted. Data entry hours dropped.

9. Telematics on transit mixers and tipper trucks: The office screen showed live location and trip counts. Idle time at the gate showed up as a number that drove conversations and fixes.

Ravi set one rule for every tool: it must export files that the firm could keep. Control sat with the owner, not 100% with the vendor.

How It Felt on the Ground

The pilot began at a new site in Kokapet. Wage day stayed in cash, but the float box sat under the site engineer's desk with a slip showing balances. The drone flew every Friday at four. The maturity sensors went into two pours in week one.

On day four, the structural engineer received a sensor log that showed the slab had reached the release threshold early. Formwork was removed by noon, and the carpentry team began work on the next shutter earlier than planned. Two days were saved without risk.

On day six, a steel supplier claimed full delivery while the gate log showed a shortfall. The RFID scan, a photo of the tag, and the store count settled the gap. The balance arrived in the evening. No temper. No blame game.

On day ten, the client for the Kokapet site asked for a quick review. The site manager shared the twin snapshot and the drone map. The payment was released through the escrow on the same night. The office did not chase calls the next day. It booked cement and blocks at better rates because cash flow was predictable.

At the end of the first month, Clara and Sudhir placed the month pack on the table. It held the Friday reconciliations, drone maps, sensor logs, invoices, and bank statements. It also had a one-page exception log with notes on how each was addressed. There was nothing for an officer to guess. There was also nothing for a buyer to doubt.

The bank manager visited again. She saw system-generated statements by site. She saw the month pack and the stage release discipline. She approved a higher limit. The public works tender for

Uppal moved to the financial opening. VK Urban Projects won one package, enough to prove that discipline and tools attract trust.

What Changed for the Firm

Vinod sat at the Kokapet site office and watched the screen. "We fight less with vendors," he said. "We have fewer reworks. We stop guessing. When the officer asks for a document, we share it without fear. I still use cash where needed. I choose where. The business is visible where it must be seen."

Ravi added a quiet line. "We did not adopt technology for style. We adopted it to receive money on time, to borrow at lower cost, and to stop telling stories when a picture will do."

Clara closed her notebook. "Audits will come," she said. "Now they will find a room that knows where each answer lives."

Cost-Benefit in Plain Words

The cost of the old paper trail was not only the tax. It was hidden time, lost discounts, blocked limits, and missed tenders. The benefit of the digital trail was not only compliance. It was stronger cash flow, fewer disputes, faster cycles, and access to larger work.

Mini-Framework for Large Contractors Who Fear the Audit Trail

- Start One Clean Lane. Select one site and apply a sweep and float type rule to keep cash levels low and predictable.

- Mirror Proof. Keep a paper and digital trail at the end of the day in a day-end PDF, so the data is duplicated.

- Use a Clean Room Device. If possible, keep banking and filing away from personal phones.

- Adopt a 4D or an advanced Model. Tie the schedule to the shape so the whole team sees the same plan.

- Build a Digital Twin. Feed it with drone maps, maturity logs, and gate receipts. Use it to trigger stage releases.

- Tag Material. Scan steel and cement on arrival, so the store count begins with a scan.

- Create Escrow Rules. Release the money on three proofs so that both sides feel secure.

- File Electronic Invoices. Tie them to the tax network and the bank.

- Automate Intake. Use a software bot to draft entries from vendor bills.

- Pack Each Month. Keep all records in a month's pack for peace of mind.

Reflection

Vinod began with a simple belief that more cash and less digital gives speed and avoids attention. That belief built his early years, and then began to shrink his circle. A large firm needs more than muscle; it requires proof on demand. The shift in Hyderabad was not a jump to shiny screens. It was a careful build of habits and tools that paid for themselves in time saved, claims avoided, limits approved, and tenders won. The ledger still matters. The twin, the model, the tags, the logs, and the month pack now stand beside it. The fear of audits did not vanish. It lost its power to freeze.

Chapter 14: "Staying Informal Saves Taxes and Gives Subsidies"

"If you think compliance is expensive, try non-compliance."

— Paul McNulty (Former U.S. Deputy Attorney General)

So, meet Ramesh. The man has been running a tiny scrap shop for ages. He's kept it very informal —no GST, no formal registration, no paperwork, none of that official stuff. Why? Well, he figures dodging the paperwork saves him money on taxes and lets him claim those sweet government benefits for small businesses. Less hassle, less spending. Can't blame him, right?

But honestly, Ramesh hasn't stopped to wonder what he's missing out on. Like, what's the catch with staying under the radar?

Why Ramesh Keeps It Informal

If you ask Ramesh, he'll straight-up tell you:

"If I register and start paying GST, and for formalisation, there goes my profit. Taxes will eat it up."

"I don't need the headache of filing returns, accounting costs, and keeping records. Way too much work."

"Plus, if I stay low-key, I still qualify for the subsidies that are supposed to help small shops like mine."

And look, he's not alone. Many small business owners believe that making things official simply means more costs and paperwork for little to no gain.

Ramesh isn't lazy or ignorant. For years, the system seemed too complicated, and the risks of going formal appeared to outweigh the rewards. But what if the reality has changed?

What He's Missing (Seriously, It's a Lot)

But here's the thing—flying under the radar isn't all sunshine and rainbows. There are a bunch of problems that come with it:

1. Can't get real loans: No paperwork, no help from the bank. So, he's stuck borrowing from sketchy sources at bonkers interest rates.

2. Big clients won't bite: The big buyers? They want GST bills and some proper business proof. Ramesh gets left with the small fry who barely pay.

3. People don't trust him: The lack of formal credentials means people see him as a risky bet. He struggles to secure any significant deals or partnerships.

All this stuff just holds him back. He's essentially running in place, not making progress.

Why Bother With Formality Anyway?

Paying taxes may sound like a pain. But going legit? It opens doors:

- Loans that don't bleed you dry: With GST and the proper documentation, banks are suddenly interested. Expansion isn't just a pipe dream.

- Bigger customers: GST bills mean he can finally chase after bulk buyers and better gigs.

- Real perks from the government: Many of the beneficial schemes and grants are only available to registered businesses in some form.

- Street cred: Being official makes him look trustworthy. People want to work with him.

Taking the Plunge, One Toe at a Time

So, Ramesh gets curious and tries something new. He signs up for GST and registers as an MSME, with the help of a consultant. Starts filing basic returns. Nothing extreme, just dipping his toes in to test the waters. He figures that maybe he doesn't have to flip his whole business overnight—just try things out and see where it goes.

"I thought I was saving ₹5000 in taxes, but I lost ₹5 lakh in contracts."

The Ladder Trick: One Rung at a Time

Think of it like climbing a ladder. First step? Register for GST or any other government registration. After that, build up your records, secure better loans, chase bigger clients, and suddenly, your business is less of a tiny shack and more of a legitimate operation.

Ramesh is up for it. He's not sprinting, but he's moving.

Final Word

For the Rameshs out there, staying informal feels like a great way to save a buck. But honestly, the real money and growth? That comes from biting the bullet—dealing with taxes and the paperwork—so you can cash in on the bigger stuff down the road. Formality isn't just some annoying expense. It's an investment, plain and simple.

Ramesh won't change overnight. But once he sees formalisation not as a tax trap, but as a **tool for trust and transformation**, things will start shifting.

For every MSME that stays small to stay safe, ask: *What are you leaving on the table?*

Sometimes, formality isn't a leap. It's just the first step to being taken seriously.

"You have to spend money to make money." — Titus Maccius Plautus.

I created a decision-making tool with simple attributes and benefits that can demonstrate to Ramesh and businesses like him what they are missing by remaining informal. You can also try this with your company or clients. I named it as;

Formalisation Return on Investment (FROI)

A **simple cost-benefit model** to estimate the ROI of Formalisation for Ramesh's business.

This tool broadly quantifies what Ramesh or businesses like him lose by staying informal, focusing on missed opportunities (loans, customers, subsidies). It uses estimates based on the scale of his scrap shop. However, this can be used for any informal or non-registered businesses. Replace with the actual figures, and feel free to add more indicators and consider sectoral variations. It's a lost opportunity calculator and not a revenue calculation tool, so the rate of interest on loan, etc, is not taken into account.

Formula:

FROI = (Expected Formal Business Gains or Estimated Loss Value – Formalisation Costs) / Formalisation Costs

Example for Ramesh:

- Expected Gains or Loss Value: ₹10 lakhs/year

- Approx. Costs: ₹50,000/year (consultant, GST, accounting)

FROI = (10,00,000 - 50,000)/50,000 = 19
→ ₹19 value unlocked for every ₹1 spent

Opportunity	Loss Value (Annual)	Assumption
Bank Loans	₹1-3 lakhs	Informal loans at a higher rate vs. bank loans at a lower rate
Bulk Buyers	₹3-5 lakhs	Revenue increases with GST invoices. Get the return and expense booking
Government Subsidies	₹50,000-1 lakh	MSME schemes (e.g., loan interest waivers)
Business Growth	₹2-3 lakh	Expansion is limited by a lack of credibility
Total Lost Value	₹6.5-12 lakh	Sum of missed opportunities

Chapter 15: The Hidden Price of Convenience

"Trust, but verify."

— Ronald Reagan

Aligarh's wholesale market was restless even after the rain. Shop shutters rattled open, puddles stretched along the drains, and men with their trousers folded to the knee carried bundles through the slush. Between a tyre repair shop and a paint supplier, Khan Packaging Solutions sat half-hidden behind stacks of flattened cartons tied with rope. Inside, boys darted around with bubble wrap, tape, and sacks of shredded paper.

Up a narrow staircase, in a small office smelling of damp paper and fresh ink, Nasir Khan sat with a ledger open in front of him. His spectacles slid down his nose as he looked up and said quietly, "Come in. I made a mistake last year, and I cannot get it out of my mind."

He began before I could ask.

"My friend in Delhi runs a big wholesale operation. He showed me the billing and inventory app he uses. It handled everything, including invoices, payments, and stock reminders. I liked it, but the cost was too high. Then I found another app online. It looked identical, had the same features, and cost less than half. I thought I was being clever. I signed up immediately and uploaded everything: my customer list, my prices, even delivery schedules."

I asked, "Did you check who owned the app or whether they had any data security certifications?"

Nasir shook his head. "No. I only looked at the features and the price. That was enough for me at the time."

The Leak

He leaned forward, lowering his voice.

"Three months later, one of my oldest clients, a chain of sweet shops, stopped ordering. I went myself to ask why. The owner said another supplier had given him the same offer I always gave: the same products, the same price, the same timing. This was not a chance. This was my private information in someone else's hands."

He sat back heavily. "I cannot prove the leak came from that app. But in twenty years of business, no one has ever copied me so precisely. And it happened only after I gave my data away."

The Missing Lock

I asked gently, "When you chose that app, did you check if the company had ISO 27001 certification?"

Nasir frowned. "What is that?"

"It is an international data security standard," I explained. "If a company has it, it means independent experts have inspected their systems and confirmed that they protect customer information. Only authorised people can access it. If a company has it, they display it proudly. If you do not see it, that is a warning sign."

Nasir's son Ayaan walked in just then with two cups of tea. He had been listening quietly and said, "Abbu, it is like giving the keys to our storeroom to someone we do not know. We never even checked if they had a shutter on their shop."

Nasir gave a tired smile. "Yes, that is exactly what I did. I bought a painted door without checking if there was a lock."

The Checklist

We opened a fresh page in his ledger and began to write. Ayaan leaned over his father's shoulder, adding points of his own.

1. Always check for ISO 27001 or similar certification.

2. Ask where the data is stored and which privacy laws apply.

3. Determine who within the company can access the data and the reasons behind this access.

4. Confirm that the data is encrypted both when stored and when sent.

5. Ensure there is an option to export or delete all data whenever needed.

Ayaan added softly, "This way, we are not trusting blindly. We are asking for proof."

The Accountant's Voice

A week later, Nasir invited his accountant, Mr. Gupta, to sit with us. The man had grey hair, a sharp memory, and a habit of adjusting his spectacles every few minutes.

Gupta listened as Nasir described the checklist. Then he said, "Data is not very different from money. You do not give your money to an unlicensed bank just because they promise a higher interest rate. In the same way, you should not give your business data to a company that cannot prove how it will keep it safe."

Nasir looked at his son. "I should have asked you both before rushing into that app."

Gupta smiled. "Better late than never. Now you know the questions to ask."

Testing the New Approach

Two weeks later, I visited again. The atmosphere in Nasir's office was different. The cooler still hummed in the corner, the cupboard still stood with its peeling paint, but Nasir himself looked lighter.

"I found another company in Pune," he said. "This time, I began with the checklist. The first thing they showed me was their ISO 27001 certificate. They explained their process in detail: every file is encrypted, only two senior managers can access it, and every action is logged. They even showed me the option to download or delete all my data at any time. My accountant reviewed the contract and said it was solid. It costs more than the old app, but this time, I know I am paying for a proper lock, not a painted door."

Ayaan, standing beside him, added proudly, "And this time, we asked the right questions first."

Mini Framework: Protecting Your Digital Data

Check This	Why It Matters	Ask This Question
ISO 27001 or equivalent certification	Proves the company meets global data safety standards	Do you have ISO 27001 or similar certification?
Data storage location	Privacy laws differ by country	Where is my data stored and under which law?

Access control	Prevents misuse inside the company	Who in your organisation can see my data and why?
Encryption	Protects data even if hacked	Is my data encrypted both when stored and sent?
Data ownership	Keeps you in control	Can I export or delete my data at any time?

Reflection

Nasir's story was not about losing money. It was about losing trust and peace of mind. The real mistake was not technology, but blind faith in a cheaper copy. Now he knows that data deserves the same protection as physical stock. Proof of safety comes before price, before features, before convenience.

Chapter 16: The Cost of Digital Intrusion

"Data is the pollution problem of the information age, and protecting privacy is the environmental challenge."

Bruce Schneier (Security Technologist)

The air in Ms Tsering's serene yoga studio in Itanagar, Arunachal Pradesh, smelled of sandalwood and peaceful intention. The natural light filtering through the large windows cast long, gentle shadows on the polished bamboo floor. For over a decade, she had built her business not on a spreadsheet, but on a foundation of trust, personal connection, and a community forged by shared breath and practice. Her students, a loyal community of locals, came to her for a sanctuary, a quiet space away from the hustle of their daily lives. Her business was an extension of her own values; it was simple, personal, and profoundly peaceful.

Yet, a growing apprehension held her back from the digital world. She saw it as the antithesis of everything she stood for. She had heard countless stories from her friends and peers about the deluge of unsolicited calls and the barrage of spam emails that came after a simple online registration. Her fear was not about technology itself, but about the intrusion that came with it. "After going digital, I will start getting calls to buy many financial and non-financial products and services because they have my data," she would lament to her lead instructor. She imagined a constant stream of automated sales pitches for yoga mats, studio equipment, and loans she didn't want or need. To her, going digital meant selling her peace of mind for an unknown benefit. The cost of convenience was a devastating loss of control over her most valuable assets: her personal space and the confidential data of her clients.

The Silent Penalty

The real price of her apprehension, however, was not the dreaded sales calls. It was the complete invisibility to professional opportunity. She had relied for years on word-of-mouth, which had been enough to keep her classes full and her business stable. But a new kind of client was emerging. The trigger came when a major private firm in the city, with a young, proactive HR team, expressed interest in hiring her for a year-long corporate wellness program. This was the kind of client that could change her business forever, offering a stable, high-value contract.

The head of their HR team, a woman named Pema, was impressed by Ms Tsering's reputation but requested a digital portfolio of her professional certifications, testimonials from past corporate clients, and a brief history of her work. Ms Tsering's professional life was a stack of physical folders filled with certificates, handwritten testimonials, and a handful of brochures. She had no professional profile, no digital footprint. Her fear of putting her data online was so strong that she couldn't bring herself to create a professional page. She believed that doing so would expose her to a world of unsolicited contact and compromise her integrity. She procrastinated, trying to find a way to deliver the information manually, but the firm's deadline passed. Her studio, competent in every other way, was not even considered for the lucrative contract. She had successfully protected her privacy, but at the far greater cost of protecting herself from a life-changing opportunity. She had been so focused on what she might lose that she had failed to see what she had already lost: her professional presence.

The New Toolkit: Choosing the Right Digital Tools

One of her clients, a technology consultant, Maya, understood Ms Tsering's fear. She knew it was a valid concern, not a simple resistance to change. She didn't push for a complete digital overhaul; she proposed a strategic shift in mindset. "The goal isn't to be everywhere, Tsering-ma. It's to be in the right places," she said, using a term of respect. Maya introduced Ms Tsering to the concept of a smart digital toolkit, a curated selection of tools chosen not for their popularity, but for their security and purpose.

Maya laid out a framework for choosing the right digital tools, focusing on the principle of 'Purpose over Promiscuity.'

1. AI-Driven Client Management: The first step was to digitalise their studio operations. Instead of a generic, public-facing payment app, Maya found a secure, cloud-based studio management software that used a modern technique called federated learning. This tool was not intended for public visibility, but rather for internal efficiency and secure record-keeping. It allowed them to manage class bookings, track attendance, and process payments without exposing client data publicly. The system's AI could even generate instant reports on her business's financial health, all while ensuring the raw data never left her system. This was the perfect solution, as the intelligence stayed with her, and the data was never at risk.

2. Token-Gated Professional Portfolio: Next, they addressed the portfolio problem. Instead of a generic social media page, they created a professional portfolio that was token-gated. Her professional credentials and client testimonials were uploaded and cryptographically signed, creating a verifiable digital record. Access to her complete portfolio was then granted to a specific, verified business partner via a unique digital token. The HR manager from the firm, for example, would receive a token-based link that would only unlock the portfolio for them. This tool enabled her to participate in the digital business world while maintaining complete control over who viewed her professional data.

3. Decentralised Communication: They replaced the public-facing phone number with a controlled communication system. Maya created a private, decentralised, end-to-end encrypted messaging channel for her community. They could send out class schedules, reminders, and updates without the fear of spam or unwanted calls. Additionally, Maya built a simple AI-powered chatbot on the studio's website that handled common inquiries (class times, pricing) automatically. This ensured her personal phone number was no longer a public asset and that her time was not consumed by answering repetitive questions.

Definitely, it was a costly implementation, but it helped Ms Tsering to be online with complete control of her information. While it was a satisfying intervention for her, many would ask why she is so concerned about her online information, considering others are not as particular as she is. But she was not only saving herself but also her clients' details from getting leaked.

The Transformation: From Apprehension to Control

A profound sense of control replaced Ms Tsering's apprehension. She realised that the digital world wasn't a single, monolithic entity, but a collection of tools, each with its own purpose and security protocols. Maya's approach wasn't about avoiding the digital world but about choosing the right tools, the ones that respected her values and her privacy.

She used her new digital toolkit to bid on the next major corporate wellness tender, this time submitting her professional portfolio on time and with confidence. She won the contract. The process was seamless, secure, and far more efficient than she could have ever imagined. She now understood that the cost of digital transformation was not a trade-off for her privacy; it was an investment in her company's security, efficiency, and future. Her data wasn't a liability to be protected, but an asset to be managed intelligently and used as a key to unlock new opportunities. She learned that a digital presence, when built with intention, could amplify her personal brand and values instead of compromising them.

Mini-Framework: Choosing Your Digital Toolkit

- **Audit Your Needs:** Before looking at any tool, step back and identify your business's core friction points. What is causing the most frustration or inefficiency? Do you need better financial management, client tracking, or professional communication? Choose a tool that solves a specific, pre-defined problem, rather than one with a list of features you may never use.

- **Prioritise Security:** Don't just look at features and price. Look for tools that prioritise data privacy, encryption, and secure access. Your client data, financial records, and personal information are your most valuable assets. A tool that compromises these assets is a liability, not an investment.

- **Start with 'Invisible' Tools:** Begin with back-end tools that don't have a public-facing component. These build your confidence without the immediate fear of exposure. Master a secure digital ledger or an internal project management system before you ever launch a public profile.

- **Evaluate Future-Proofing:** Ask vendors about their security protocols, data storage location, and interoperability with other systems. A good tool should be a long-term partner, not a quick fix that will become obsolete or insecure in a few years.

Chapter 17: Guarding the Crown Jewels

"It takes 20 years to build a reputation and five minutes to ruin it. If you think about that, you'll do things differently."

— Warren Buffett

In Surat's Mahidharpura market, business starts before the city does. By eight o'clock, men in pastel shirts and neatly pressed trousers are already bending over long wooden tables, peeking at stones under white lamps. The sound here is soft, a loupe clicking shut, diamonds dropping into felt trays, the muted hum of polishing wheels from upstairs rooms.

On the second floor of a weathered building with peeling paint, a brass nameplate reads *Vraj Gems*. Inside, the air smells faintly of oil and stone dust. Four polishers sit in a row, each with a spinning wheel in front of them, their movements precise and unhurried.

At the far end, behind a heavy desk, sits Bharat Vraj. In front of him is a thick account register, its corners curled from years of turning. This register is more than paper and ink; it's his pricing book, his deal history, his private strategy.

When I walked in, he didn't look up right away. He finished writing a figure, underlined it twice, and only then pushed a steel glass of chai toward me.

"Before you start," he said, "let me be clear. If going digital means my prices end up where others can see them, I'm not interested.

These numbers," he tapped the register, "are my life's work. You're asking me to put them into someone else's machine? No chance."

Why the Fear Runs Deep

Bharat's worry didn't come from nowhere. Two years earlier, another workshop in his building had started using a flashy online inventory platform. Six months later, whispers spread that one of their competitors had matched their pricing to the last rupee.

"No one could prove it," Bharat said, "but in this business, if your prices leak, you don't just lose deals, you lose trust. Clients think you're careless. Traders stop calling."

For him, pricing wasn't just a number. It was a carefully balanced mix of stone quality, market timing, a guarded secret sauce and personal relationship with each client. Revealing it was like giving away the secret recipe of a family sweet shop.

I didn't argue. Instead, I asked, "What if going digital didn't mean sharing your prices, what if it meant making sure no one else could see them?"

He frowned. "You mean hiding them inside the system?"

"Exactly. We can set up tools where only you have the password to the pricing file. Your staff will see only what they need: polishing deadlines, delivery dates, and stone weights, with no information about your rates. Even if someone tried, there would be nothing for them to copy. All encrypted and secured"

Bharat called his nephew Rikin, who managed email orders. "Explain this to him," he said.

Rikin nodded. "Kaka, it's like the workshop key. The polishers can enter the polishing room, but not your office. In the software, we provide access in the same way: one key for polishing jobs and another for prices. You keep the second one."

Bharat agreed to try, but only if there was no risk. For one month, they would put *only non-pricing details* into the system: job number, client initials, delivery date, and stone weight. Prices would remain in his register.

The polishers' routine didn't change. But Rikin no longer had to run up and down the stairs to confirm which parcels were due next. The software showed him the day's pending jobs, and he passed the details to each polisher without touching pricing.

Midway through the trial, a Hong Kong client asked for updates on three parcels. Usually, Bharat would stop what he was doing, flip through the register, call the polishing room, and then call the client back. This time, Rikin checked the job list, confirmed the status, and replied within minutes, while Bharat kept working undisturbed.

Choosing the Right Tool

At the end of the month, Bharat was ready to consider a permanent solution, but only on his terms. Together, he and Rikin looked at three options. They rejected the non-certified apps immediately, "Too risky to share data, " Bharat said.

They finally chose a reputable company with all data certifications, encryption, etc, that understood the trade's need for confidentiality. The system included:

- **User-level permissions** so pricing screens were visible only to Bharat.

- **Local storage** with daily backup to a hard drive in Bharat's office.

- **Offline access** allows them to keep working during internet outages.

- **Complete export control**, so Bharat could take his data anytime without asking anyone's permission.

- Option to delete the data completely whenever he wants to stop using the tool. No data retention after exit. Similar to a clean entry, he wanted a clean exit, too.

The Pressure Test

The real test came during the December wedding rush. A Mumbai trader placed a large, urgent order and wanted progress updates every two days.

In the past, Bharat would have had to call the polishing room repeatedly, each time risking that someone overheard client details they didn't need to know.

Now, Rikin checked the system for job completion status and sent updates, without mentioning prices or touching sensitive files. Bharat prepared the invoice himself when the job was done, the numbers never leaving his desk.

The trader complimented their speed. Bharat said nothing, but later, over chai, he admitted, "It worked. We moved faster, and no one saw what they shouldn't." I shared with him the case of Nasir Khan from Aligarh, who was also quite sensitive about his business data and how his data got leaked, as well as the ISO standards on data protection, both for business and personal purposes.

Mini-Framework: Protecting Strategy While Going Digital

Bharat was quite informative and put in extra efforts to ensure that the data is secured and in control. But what about other Bharats? Can we come up with a checklist?

Step	Action	Why It Matters
1	List your sensitive data	Know what must stay private (pricing, supplier rates, client lists)
2	Choose tools with access control	Ensure each user sees only what they need
3	Prefer local or hybrid storage	Reduces exposure to unknown servers
4	Keep offline backups	Maintains control even if the system fails
5	Start with non-sensitive data	Builds trust before adding confidential details
6	Check, delete at your will, and have the right to be forgotten.	Check if the application has data protection certifications. And what are their policies on data deletion after you have deleted your account?

Reflection

Bharat's fear wasn't of technology; it was of losing the control that kept his business alive. By starting small, setting clear boundaries, and choosing a system built for his reality, he learned that digital could serve him without stripping away his privacy.

The prices are still in that thick register on his desk. But now, the rest of the work, tracking jobs, meeting deadlines, and updating clients, happens faster, cleaner, and with fewer interruptions. The crown jewels stay locked, yet the workshop runs sharper than ever.

Section 3: Practical Barriers & Misconceptions

Beyond money and fear, there are very real practical barriers. MSMEs struggle with poor internet, language barriers, bargaining culture, and the perception that digital lacks the warmth of chai-biscuits conversations. Many also confuse "using WhatsApp" with being digital-ready. This section clears those clouds and shows how simple, context-specific digital solutions can work even in small towns, low-income setups, and traditional industries.

Chapter 18: The Amplifier in Your Hands

"Technology should not overpower tradition. It should support it, the way light supports a mirror to show what is already there."

- *Dr. A P J Abdul Kalam*

The lanes of Aminabad in Lucknow never lose their energy. Rickshaws move past each other with inches to spare, hawkers call out to customers, and the smell of freshly fried kachoris mingles with the sweetness of jalebis. Inside one of those lanes stood Royal Bakery, a modest shop that had served bread, rusks, and cakes for over three decades. The shopfront was simple, with glass shelves full of biscuits and a wooden counter where the owner, Ramesh Agarwal, sat with his notebook open.

Ramesh had inherited the business from his father. The bakery was well known among nearby families, and during festivals, people queued up for his plum cakes and butter biscuits. Yet despite the steady flow of customers, he felt uneasy whenever the subject of digital systems came up.

I asked him once why he avoided them. He closed his notebook and looked me straight in the eye.

"Sir, I have worked this way for thirty years. I know my customers by face. I note everything by hand. If I go digital, I will depend on a software company. They will update, change, or stop working, and then I will be helpless. At least here, with my pen and paper, I am in control."

At the back of the shop, his young assistant, Sameer, arranged trays of biscuits. He glanced up at his employer and smiled faintly but said nothing. He had tried more than once to introduce a simple billing tool, but Ramesh always dismissed the idea.

The Familiar Notebook

Ramesh turned the notebook toward me. The pages were filled with neat handwriting, listing orders for bread and cakes. He tapped on the lines as he spoke.

"See, this family has been with us for twenty years. They call me directly. I write it here. During Diwali, I make a note of the date for cake delivery. Sometimes an order gets misplaced, yes, but I handle it. What if the same happened in a digital system? I would not even know how to correct it."

I asked gently, "And when an order is misplaced, what do you do?"

He sighed. "Either I refund the amount, or I give extra biscuits to make peace. Last year, during Diwali, I lost nearly fifteen thousand rupees this way."

Sameer finally spoke. "Sir, if we had digital records, it would remind us of pending orders. We would not miss them."

Ramesh shook his head. "And if the phone stops working? Or if the company asks for more payment? At least my notebook never betrays me."

A Memory of Change

To ease the tension, I asked him about the bakery's early years.

115

"Ramesh ji, when you first introduced the electric mixer for kneading dough, how did you feel?"

He chuckled. "I remember it well. My father opposed it. He trusted only hand kneading. He said machines spoil the texture. But as orders grew, we had no choice. The mixer saved time, and the taste remained the same."

"So the recipe was still yours," I said, "but the tool made the work faster."

Ramesh rubbed his chin thoughtfully. "You are saying digital is like that mixer."

"Yes. The mixer does not bake the cake. It only prepares the dough better. Similarly, digital technology does not run your bakery. It only helps you manage orders and stock better."

A Small Experiment

Sameer was quick to seize the opening. He took out his phone and showed a simple app where he had entered a few trial orders.

"This is only for cakes," he explained. "Nothing else. Let me enter Holi orders here. You keep writing in your notebook. I will do the digital entry separately. If it fails, your notebook remains."

Ramesh frowned but allowed it, more out of indulgence than conviction.

For the next week, nothing changed. Ramesh wrote diligently in his notebook. Sameer entered the exact details into the app. When a customer called, Ramesh flipped through pages while Sameer tapped his screen.

Then one morning, as the festival season approached, Sameer showed the phone to his employer. "Sir, look at this list. Fifteen cakes are due today. Six items are available for pickup, and nine

116

items are available for delivery. All names and dates are here in one view."

Ramesh stared silently. His notebook had the exact details, but scattered across different pages. It would have taken him half an hour to compile the same list.

The Turning Point

During Holi, when the rush peaked, the app sent reminders each morning. No order was missed. No refund was required. When the season ended, Ramesh calculated his earnings.

"This year," he admitted slowly, "we saved almost twenty thousand rupees in mistakes. Perhaps it is not so bad after all."

Still, he clung to his notebook. "I like paper. It feels real. Phones feel borrowed. What if they stop tomorrow?"

I told him, "It is good to keep your notebook. But see this for what it is. Digital is not taking over your bakery. It is supporting you, just like the mixer supported your hands. You still bake, greet customers, and make decisions. The app only reflects your work more clearly."

Ramesh nodded reluctantly. "So I remain the baker. The tool only helps me avoid foolish losses."

Extending the Use

Encouraged, Sameer suggested trying the same system for raw materials. "Sir, every festival we either run short of sugar and butter, or we overstock dry fruits and then sell them at a discount later. If we record purchases, we will know exactly what is lying in the storeroom."

Ramesh resisted at first. But after one season, when he lost money selling old almonds at a throwaway price, he agreed. Within two months, the system showed him precise numbers. He began planning purchases better.

Later, he admitted, "I thought digital would make me dependent on outsiders. But it has reduced my dependence. Earlier, I relied on memory and guesswork. Now I rely on figures I can see clearly."

The Lesson of Amplification

For Ramesh, the bakery was never about technology. It was about trust, reputation, and recipes passed down from his father. He feared that digital would disturb that balance.

But his experience showed otherwise.

- His notebook still existed, but the system amplified accuracy.

- His recipes remained unchanged, but planning improved.

- His relationships with customers remained intact, but reliability increased.

Digital did not take away his craft. It amplified it.

Mini Framework: Using Digital as an Amplifier in Food Businesses

1. Start with one process. Begin with order tracking or inventory management before attempting anything else.

2. Keep both systems. Use a notebook and digital side-by-side until trust is built.

3. Let someone younger handle it. Assign an employee or family member as the digital caretaker.

4. Measure the benefit. Track the money saved from fewer mistakes or less wastage.

5. Expand step by step. Add new functions only after the first becomes comfortable.

Reflection

Royal Bakery did not transform overnight. Ramesh still sits at his wooden counter, notebook open, greeting familiar faces. He still believes in personal relationships and the feel of paper in hand. But alongside the notebook is a quiet companion that counts faster, reminds him sooner, and prevents costly errors.

The journey was not about surrender. It was about amplification. Digital did not replace his way of working. It gave it sharper edges and fewer leaks.

Chapter 19: The Myth About "Later"

"Don't wait. The time will never be just right."

— Napoleon Hill

It was early in Morbi's ceramic district, but the day had already started. Trucks carrying stacks of tiles rumbled past on the main road, their drivers calling out to each other as they slowed to avoid potholes. The air smelled of clay and smoke from kilns that had been burning since before dawn. On one corner, workers crowded around a tea stall, holding small glasses of thick, sweet chai.

Rajeshbhai's workshop was at the very end of a narrow lane. From outside, it looked like nothing more than a large shed with a faded blue signboard, Shree Krishna Ceramic Moulds. Inside, it was alive with movement. Two men poured clay into moulds, another smoothed the edges of half-formed tiles, and a fourth carried trays of finished pieces to dry in the sun outside. The hum of the polishing wheel mixed with the rhythmic thud of someone stacking moulds.

Rajeshbhai stood near the main workbench, his sleeves rolled up and a thin layer of clay dust clinging to his forearms. He noticed me at the entrance and waved me in.

"You're here just in time," he said. "Tea?"

We sat at a small desk near the corner, where a steel cupboard leaned heavily against the wall. Rajeshbhai spoke without much prompting.

"Everyone tells me I should invest in digital. Track my orders, manage my accounts effectively, and potentially promote my work online. I always tell them the same thing. First, I need to earn more money. When I have extra profits, I will review them. Right now, I cannot spend on things that do not make tiles."

I asked him, "And you are sure digital will not make more tiles?"

He smiled slightly. "I have been in this line for more than twenty years. I can recall from memory which orders are late, which suppliers are slow, and which clients take the longest to pay. I do not need an app for that."

Before I could respond, a worker walked over holding a crumpled slip of paper.

A Problem in Real Time

"Sir, this order for Patel Tiles," the worker began, "did we send two hundred pieces last week or not? The file is missing."

Rajeshbhai frowned. "Check the drawer on the right."

"I did," the worker said. "Nothing there."

"Then call Ramesh at the loading dock," Rajeshbhai replied. "He might remember."

As the worker left, Rajeshbhai sighed. "This is the sort of nonsense that slows me down. But still, these things happen."

I leaned forward. "This is exactly why you cannot wait until 'later'. Every time you spend minutes or hours chasing information, you are losing both time and money. And that is before counting the mistakes that come from guesswork."

He looked at me carefully, as if trying to decide whether I was making a sales pitch.

121

"I am not talking about expensive systems," I said. "I am talking about starting small, right now, with tools that cost nothing and still save you time."

I asked him to take out his phone. "Let us make a simple record. Just three things: order number, quantity, and delivery date."

He unlocked the phone and handed it over. I opened Google Sheets, typed in the headings, and added the Patel Tiles order first. Then we added two more orders from his notebook.

"You can share this with Mahesh and your supervisor," I explained. "They can update it from their own phones. Next time someone asks about an order, you open this sheet and see the answer in seconds."

Rajeshbhai tapped the screen a couple of times. "This is free?"

"Yes," I said. "And it works on any phone."

The Festival Rush Test

Three weeks later, I visited again. The workshop was a whirl of activity. The Diwali rush had begun. Orders were stacked against the wall, trucks were waiting outside, and two customers had come in person to collect their shipments.

In the middle of all this, a supplier called to confirm an old order. Rajeshbhai reached for his phone, opened the sheet, and within seconds told him the exact dispatch date and truck number.

He looked up at me and grinned. "This would have been a half-hour job before."

Why "Later" is Too Late

As we stepped outside for tea, Rajeshbhai said, "I always thought I would wait until I had more money. Now I see that digital is not something you buy after you succeed. It is something that helps you succeed; it should gradually become a part of your daily activities."

He stirred his tea slowly. "Even this small sheet has saved me at least a day's worth of trouble in the last month. And when you run a small workshop, a day saved is a lot of money saved."

Mini Framework: Start Digital Before You Think You Can

Step	Action	Why It Matters
1	Pick one simple process to track digitally	Avoids overload, builds early wins
2	Use free tools to start	Removes cost barrier
3	Share access with one or two trusted people	Reduces dependency on memory and your availability
4	Check updates weekly	Helps you spot delays and losses early
5	Upgrade only when the current system feels too small	Ensures spending is justified

Reflection

Rajeshbhai began with the belief that digital was an investment for later. However, by starting with something free and simple, he realised it was an investment for the present. He understood that digital tools are not a reward for success; they are the pathway to it.

Chapter 20: Who Holds the Remote?

"Trust, but verify."

- **Ronald Reagan**

At dawn, Jaipur's Transport Nagar sounded like a hundred kettles whistling at once. Diesel engines coughed awake, tarpaulin sheets slapped against truck bodies, and a tea boy moved between parked rigs with a kettle swinging from his arm. Under a tin roof near a puncture shop, a small office carried a hand-painted board: "Khalsa Desert Carriers." Inside were two steel almirahs, a glass-topped table with a crack across the corner, and three registers stacked like bricks.

Gurmeet Kaur owned the fleet. Ten rigid trucks hauled marble from Kishangarh, spices from Chandpole Bazaar, and occasionally textile bales to the NCR. She waved me in, offered tea, and pointed at the registers.

"You have come to talk about digital," she said in Hindi. "I will tell you straight. I do not like the idea. If I go digital, some company will hold my data. They will keep charging. If their systems break, my trucks will stand still. With these books, I am in control."

A young dispatcher, Imran, sat at a side table drawing a route map with a blue pen. Two drivers, Bhanwar and Harpreet, checked a list of tolls and fuel halts. The morning felt like a play where everyone knew their lines.

Gurmeet flipped open a register. Every page displayed the date, truck number, loading point, unloading point, diesel issued, and a separate box for advances. "A transporter in Sitapura signed up for a fancy transport management system last year," she said. "Real-time tracking, invoicing, e-way bill reminders, all that. For six months, he was proud. Then the company increased the fee and removed the cheaper plan. He was unable to export his full data. He spent nights copying things by hand. Tell me, why should I give a stranger the steering?"

Her words carried the core fear. For her, digital did not mean learning a new tool. It meant surrendering control to an outsider.

I asked, "Gurmeet ji, when you pass a toll, you use FASTag. You do not control that system either, yet you accept it because traffic flows."

"That is different," she said. "If one toll gate malfunctions, I still have nine more on the route. If a software company fails, everything fails at once. And I cannot change suppliers overnight."

A parallel worry from another businesswoman

Later that week, I stopped in Ajmer to meet Rekha Jacob, who ran a small courier kiosk near the railway station. She shipped parcels for coaching students and small shops. One wall displayed a picture of Sacred Heart and a calendar with church feast days marked in blue.

"I tried an invoicing app," she said, smiling wearily. "After two months, it asked me to upgrade to print the same label in bulk. I did not find the application worth upgrading, so I deleted it. I know, like me, they are also in business and need revenue, but it wasn't worth the upgrade. My manual receipt book never tells me to pay more."

The scale was tiny compared to Gurmeet's hundred-tonne weeks, but the emotion was identical. Digital felt like a remote control in someone else's hand.

A new way to frame control

Back in Jaipur, I sat with Gurmeet as drivers queued for diesel slips.

"Let me try your language," I said. "On the highway, the dashboard shows speed, temperature, and fuel. Does the dashboard drive the truck?"

"No," she said, half smiling.

"GPS and apps are dashboards. They do not turn the wheel. They reflect what your drivers do. If one dashboard fails, the truck can still move. Your job is to make sure the dashboard never becomes the wheel. For that, you keep the keys: your data and your knowledge."

She listened without interrupting. Imran raised his eyebrows but kept quiet.

I told her about a transporter in Jodhpur that carried sandstone. They refused to sign a single, comprehensive contract. Instead, they used three small tools. One free app for trip sheets, another for invoicing, and a simple weekly backup to their own Google Drive. Every Friday evening, they exported Excel files and a PDF summary. If any vendor misbehaved, they could be switched without losing their history.

Gurmeet leaned forward. "So it is not all or nothing. You can keep modules separate and keep copies yourself."

"That is the principle," I said. "Keep the steering in your hands. Let the dash light up, but never let it hold the wheel."

"However, if you get a single application that is worth the premium upgrade and rich in features that you want, you must consider buying it, so that all your information and insight is in one place. Multiple apps are good for when you are starting up or have a very simple and specific requirement, but when you use them for scale, it is always recommended to buy a paid version."

Building control inside the room

Dependency grows when nobody inside understands the system. Once even one person learns, control returns. Rekha, the courier, trained her nephew to set up a basic spreadsheet. He printed a monthly summary that matched her receipt book. "Now I show this to the courier company when they calculate dues," she said later. "I do not feel at their mercy."

In Gurmeet's office, Imran had the curiosity and patience to be the internal champion. She agreed, reluctantly, to a one-month trial with three guardrails. No long contracts. All data is exportable as files. And registers would run in parallel until she felt safe.

Imran set up a lean workflow.

1. A trip sheet app with only four fields: truck, origin, destination, and committed delivery date.

2. A separate invoicing tool to generate bills and mail PDFs to clients.

3. A weekly backup ritual every Friday at six. He exported CSVs and PDFs to a folder named "Khalsa_Baselines," then copied it to a pen drive Gurmeet kept in her almirah.

No live tracking, no complex dashboards. This was a mirror, not a remote.

On day two, a client from Gurgaon called three times to ask for the truck's location. Earlier, Imran would dial Bhanwar, who would then shout into the wind and name a dhaba as a landmark. Now, Imran sent a WhatsApp live location link that expired in eight hours. The client was satisfied. Imran felt clever.

On day four, the e-way bill portal was slow. Imran panicked and reached for the new apps. Nothing there could help. He returned to the old paper printout and the driver's laminated instruction sheet, which explained what to do at a checkpoint. That day, the dashboard was truly just a dashboard. The truck moved because the basics still worked.

At week's end, Gurmeet opened the register to reconcile advances. Imran placed two printouts next to it. One showed trips by truck number with committed and actual delivery dates. The second showed pending invoices by client.

Gurmeet's finger stopped at a number. "This client gives detention-free hours of two. We delivered in five, yet we wrote off detention. Why?"

Imran called Harpreet. He described a temple procession that had blocked a city corner for an hour. "I did not want to sound like I was making excuses," Harpreet said.

Gurmeet drew a small circle around the trip ID. "We need proof for detention. Next time, click one photo of the jam and add it to the trip. If the client declines, I will still know we were not lazy."

Imran added "photo note" to the trip checklist. Control was becoming practice.

On Monday, a salesperson from a logistics SaaS firm walked in with a laptop bag and offered an all-in-one platform. "You will get driver scorecards, RFID trip tags, RTO reminders, and a beautiful control tower," he said, sliding a slick demo across the table.

Gurmeet smiled. "Can I export all data anytime?" she asked.

"Of course," he said. "You can request an export."

"Request means wait," she replied. "I want a button."

The salesperson promised to check with his team and left a trial link. Gurmeet did not open it.

That afternoon, a client delayed payment again. Imran pulled up invoices mailed over the last thirty days with delivery proofs attached. The client agreed to clear two bills immediately because the bundle looked complete.

By week three, the team added small pieces.

- Driver codes on the trip sheet so that advances could be tallied by person, not only by truck.

- A one-page SOP taped near the window that read: "If app fails, do the trip. Save notes on paper. Export Friday."

- A red dot on the trip list for any load where the due date was inside 24 hours. Imran stopped guessing which call to return first.

Harpreet suggested a trick. "If you send me the client's name and delivery promise by message, I do not have to call you each time the gatekeeper stops me. I will show the message."

Imran began sending a single-line message at loading: "Client: Arora Marble, Deliver by: 24th noon." The gatekeepers stopped arguing about vague commitments. A sentence had replaced ten calls.

At the end of the month, Gurmeet closed the registers with a less tight jaw. The experiment had not made the road smoother. It had made the office clearer.

"What changed?" I asked.

Imran read from a small notebook.

- Fewer repeated calls. Live location links and one-line promises reduced chatter.

- Faster invoicing. PDFs sent the same evening meant fewer disputes over rates and loading dates.

- Detention visibility. Two trips received partial detention because the photo note made the case easier.

- No lock-in. All files were stored on the almirah pen drive as well as in a shared folder.

Gurmeet added her own line. "I still trust my registers. But now I know that the register is not the only place where my business lives. My business lives in the choices I make. The tools are just lights." She also requested that I refer her to a few applications worth considering for the premium upgraded plan, as she is now more confident of using the applications for her business.

Mini Framework: Keep the Steering With You

1. Own your data.

Use tools that let you export CSVs and PDFs with one click at your command. Back them up to places you control every week.

2. Build an internal champion.

Train one to two trusted staff members or family members. It's okay to pay them for the extra responsibility. Knowledge inside reduces fear outside.

3. Go modular.

To start with, a trip sheet in one tool, invoicing in another, backups in a third. If one fails, the business still moves. However, for the long term, consider purchasing a premium plan for a good application; it's worth the investment.

4. Avoid long lock-ins.

Prefer monthly plans or free tiers. Read the exit path before the entry form. After you become confident, you may choose yearly plans; mostly, they will be cheaper.

5. Write a paper fallback.

Keep a one-page SOP for when the network goes down or a portal is unavailable. Your process should run without permission from a server.

6. Document friction.

Add a quick photo note for jams and loading delays. Detention pays once it teaches clients to respect time.

7. Audit once a week.

Reconcile register totals with exports every Friday. Control is a habit, not a feeling.

Reflection

Every business depends on others. Gurmeet depends on quarries releasing stone on time, on pumps dispensing clean diesel, on police not stopping trucks without cause, and on buyers paying as promised. Technology is simply another dependence in that list. The mistake is to hand the steering to a dashboard. The correction is to keep knowledge and data in the owner's room.

Gurmeet began with a fear that some company would hold the remote. A month later, the remote looked smaller. She had a pen drive with her history, a routine for exports, and a dispatcher who could read numbers as well as he could read the road. The trucks continued to roll on the same highways. The difference was in the office. Fewer arguments. Fewer loops. A little more sleep.

As we stepped out, Bhanwar started his engine, and a faint saffron of dust rose from the yard. "The dashboard can talk," Gurmeet said, half to herself, "but the wheel stays with us."

Chapter 21: Speaking the Language of Business

"If you talk to a man in a language he understands, that goes to his head. If you talk to him in his own language that goes to his heart."

- **Nelson Mandela**

Cuttack wakes early to the clink of tiny hammers. In a narrow lane behind Choudhury Bazar, I visited a silver filigree workshop, the kind that has worked for generations in this city. Fine silver wire looped like vines on wooden boards. A charcoal stove breathed softly in the corner. On a low cot sat Sabina Begum, a master craftswoman, shaping a pair of peacock earrings no bigger than a thumbnail. Her younger sister, Farzana, sat beside her, twisting strands of wire into delicate coils. On the shelf lay small packets of silver, each marked by weight in grams. Orders came from local shops and from a trader in Bhubaneswar who collected finished pieces every fortnight.

I asked Sabina if she had considered using a mobile app to record orders and track silver usage. She stopped the movement of her tool and gave me a wary smile.

"I tried once," she said. "The app was in English. My reading is in Odia. The screen filled with words that did not feel natural to me. I know some English, but what if I press the wrong button? Will I lose money or make an incorrect entry? My diary cannot betray me."

Farzana added without looking up, "We handle money, stock, and pay karigars on time. We bargain, cost, and deliver. We are not afraid of work. However, these apps seem to be designed for others. People who live in offices, not in rooms like this."

Their fear was not of technology. It was in language. The worry arrived before the first tap on the glass.

I asked Sabina a question I had asked many times. "When you learned your first filigree pattern, did you get it right at once?"

She laughed. "Never. My first 'jhilmil' flower looked like a crushed ant. My mother told me to start again. I started again until my hand understood."

"So why does a phone feel different?" I asked.

"Because the phone looks like someone else's world," she said. "Here, if I make a mistake, I can melt the silver and try again. On the phone, it feels like I will break something I cannot fix."

Her nephew Kabir, a college student who had been sorting tiny stones, looked up. "Khalamma, many apps now allow Odia. You choose once in Settings, and it stays. Even if the app is in English, the phone can read for you. You can speak, and it will write. You can point the camera at a word and it will show Odia."

Sabina frowned. "Last year, I downloaded one app. Only English and Odia translations looked like another language. I deleted it the same day. I do not want that stress."

A small demonstration

I unlocked my phone and opened a simple order book app, which I use for such demonstrations. I showed the language settings and switched to Odia. The labels changed at once. Quantity, price, save, share, all appeared in the script she used to write lists for the market. Then I handed over the phone to her.

Sabina tapped and started exploring it, maybe trying to find if this works or to find a point to justify the "I told you" moment. "So it can speak to me," she said.

I showed two more tricks. Opened the keyboard microphone and spoke a line in Odia. The phone typed the sentence. Then he pointed the camera at an English invoice from the Bhubaneswar trader. The live translation overlaid Odia words on top of the page.

Farzana leaned closer. "You mean even if the app is in English, we can still read in Odia?"

"Not perfectly," I said, "but enough to begin. The phone can bend more than we think."

The hesitation of the first step

We agreed to test only one thing. I helped Kabir set up a single-page titled "Daily Orders." He created three fields with large buttons. Buyer name, design code, and pieces. I took a promise not to explore other features until they are comfortable.

Sabina entered her first line. She looked for the peacock earrings in a list, could not find them, and grew tense. "See. It is already going wrong," she said.

I said. "You do not have to search. Just speak. Say 'Mor Pankha 2' and press save."

She spoke. The line appeared as a short code that they had agreed on: MP for Mor Pankha, and the number. She stared at it and then at the shelf where the silver packets lay. The code felt like a bridge between her world and the screen.

135

The next morning, she forgot to press save and lost the entry. She was annoyed with herself. On the third day, she entered three lines in a row and checked them twice. By the end of the week, she could enter orders without help. She was not ready for costing or stock reconciliation, but the fear had become a smaller animal.

The quiet power of numbers

That evening, while the stove cooled and the tiny peacocks rested on a tray, Sabina said something that stayed with me. "I thought digital meant English. It actually means numbers. Numbers are my language. I count grams. I price stones. If the phone can stay in numbers, I can walk with it."

That one sentence carried her whole journey. The barrier was not willingness or talent. It was the fear that she would be excluded before she began. When the phone met her halfway, she walked the rest.

We turned the single page into a slightly stronger tool without adding clutter.

1. Design codes that felt like home. Instead of long English names, they set short codes that matched how the workshop spoke. MP for Mor Pankha, CK for Chakri, GC for Ghunghroo Chain. No searching through foreign lists.

2. Pieces first, grams later. The first screen asked only for the buyer's name and the number of pieces. A second, optional screen lets them record silver in grams. Sabina decided to use it only twice a day. She did not want a phone near hot charcoal.

3. Colour hints. Urgent orders appeared in red—regular orders in blue. Anything completed turned green. Farzana said the colours reminded her of the thread spools they used to tie bundles.

4. Voice, not typing. The microphone button stayed on the top left. Sabina spoke in Odia. The numbers and codes appeared with one or two mistakes at first, then improved as the phone learned her voice. With Artificial Intelligence (AI), tools have become smarter, enabling them to predict trends and provide valuable insights.

5. One backup that did not frighten them. Every evening, Kabir pressed a single share button and sent a PDF of the day's orders to his own WhatsApp. Sabina liked the idea that her entries were stored in both the phone and a message thread she could open and show to a buyer.

Language in the market

The following week, Peter Nayak came from CTC Silver, a small showroom near Buxi Bazaar. He placed his order while sipping tea. As he spoke, Sabina recorded each line on the phone. When he asked for a copy, she tapped share, and the day's list travelled to his number at once.

Peter looked surprised. "Sabina ji, you have become very high tech," he joked. "Earlier, you used to call me three times about pieces."

Sabina smiled. "Now the phone listens to my Odia. If it forgets, the list remembers."

Later that day, another export buyer, Zubin Wadia, called from Mumbai. He wanted photographs of a new bracelet. Kabir took two pictures, added the code ZB Brace01, and shared the image with the code typed in Odia and English. Zubin replied with a thumbs-up and a date for pickup. The workshop felt, for the first time, that the phone had become a courier for their craft rather than a judge of their English.

The second fear

A week later, new hesitations appeared. Sabina worried that the trader would now expect her to maintain full accounts on the phone. She was willing to record orders, but not ready to replace her diary.

We set a guardrail. The phone would run only two functions for a month. Daily orders and a simple summary for each buyer at the end of the week—no promises beyond that. When a tool grows too fast, trust shrinks.

I explained to Kabir to print the small print button for the mobile app-based invoices. On Fridays, he printed a single page with buyer-wise counts and gave it to Sabina's trader. The trader liked it because he no longer had to cross-check every item in her diary. Sabina liked it because the diary remained the final book. The phone simply made the diary clean.

What changed and what did not?

I called back to check the progress after a few weeks, and I asked,

"What changed?"

"We argue less," she said. "When someone says you promised six pairs and we think we made four, we open the list and see. And I spend less time reading back old pages."

"We waste fewer scraps because we cut to the count. Earlier, we made an extra piece to be on the safe side. Now we make it to the line."

But, Sabina still does costing on paper. But this phone app has learned to sit quietly without shouting in English."

She had one more request. "Teach me camera translation again. The silver supplier's price list comes in English. If I can read it in Odia, I will not ask Kabir each time."

We got onto a video call, and she tried it three more times until she could keep the camera steady and tap pause when the Odia overlay was correct. Each time she translated a price, the worry in her face loosened a little.

Mini framework: when language blocks digital for micro businesses

1. Start with a single page. One screen with two or three buttons that map to daily work. No extra features during the first month.

2. Make codes that match speech. Use short names or codes that the team already uses. Avoid foreign lists and long menus.

3. Use voice as the default. Enable voice typing in the local language. Let the user speak numbers and short codes.

4. Lean on camera translation. For invoices and menus that arrive in English, use the camera to overlay Odia, Assamese, or any supported script.

5. Teach only what pays today. In craft businesses, start with orders and pieces. Add costing or stock later.

6. Back up in a friendly way. Share a daily PDF on a WhatsApp group with yourself or with other partners or a family member. Visible, simple, quick.

7. Set guardrails. Tell buyers that digital records support the diary; they do not replace it yet. Expand only after calm is achieved.

8. More than just records and bookkeeping. Such tools are powerful and smart with AI. Do not use them only for stock or invoices, but to explore loans, payments, and sell

online, etc. Also, use it to get insights and predictions on your business.

Reflection

For many micro entrepreneurs, the locked door is not the price of a phone or the lack of data. It is language. A screen in English can make a master craftswoman feel like a visitor in her own shop. What opened the door in Sabina's room was not a complicated system. It was a page that respected her words. The phone learned her codes. She did not have to know someone else's.

Adoption did not begin with the whole app. It started with a number and a save button. The room's rhythm did not break. Her diary did not vanish. But arguments reduced, waste fell, and buyers received clear summaries on time. The craft remained the centre. Digital came closer, took off its shoes, and sat on the floor.

Chapter 22: When the Net Stops, the Work Must Go On

"Do what you can, with what you have, where you are."

— Theodore Roosevelt

The road into Dobhi, Himachal Pradesh, narrowed into a stony path that sloped down toward the river. On one side were bare apple trees, their branches black against the pale sky; on the other, small homes with carved wooden balconies.

I could hear it before I saw it, the rhythmic "tak-tak" of wooden pedals and the soft swoosh of wool sliding through the warp.

Inside Nisha Wool Works, four women sat at traditional looms, their shawls growing inch by inch. Wool bundles lay piled in one corner, crimson, saffron, mustard yellow — each colour telling you which natural dye bath it had come from. The air was warm from the tandoor stove in the corner, faintly scented with lanolin from the wool.

Nisha herself was perched on a low stool near the counter, her hair tied in a neat braid, a measuring tape looped around her neck. She was rolling up a finished Kullu shawl, her fingers running along the edges as if checking every thread for loyalty.

She looked up and smiled, "You made it early. The tea is still on the stove."

As we waited, I asked how the business was going. Her smile faded.

"Good work, bad reach," she said. "We weave beautiful pieces, buyers from Delhi and Chandigarh know our name... but the network here plays hide and seek."

Her voice carried frustration that came from more than one bad incident. She continued:

"Last month, a boutique owner called, big order, ten shawls. I had them ready to photograph. I took the pictures, pressed send, and that was it - a spinning wheel on the screen. The internet was gone. I kept checking every few minutes, moving around the workshop to catch a signal. By the time it came back, she had already got the rates from someone else. I not only missed the opportunity to be the first to share the product and rate, which would have led to a sale, but I also felt less efficient and careless, as she might be thinking. "By the time she received my message, she had already placed the order with someone else as she wanted the products to be delivered quickly."

She poured tea into glasses and slid one across the table. "Tell me honestly, how will any digital tool help me if I can't even get a bar of signal?"

I asked how she kept track of orders. She reached under the counter and pulled out a thick, cloth-bound notebook.

"Everything is here," she said, flipping through pages neatly divided into columns. "Date, buyer's name, quantity, payment. If this gets wet or lost, I will not even remember half the details."

She laughed bitterly. "My husband tells me to 'go modern'. But modern doesn't walk up this mountain."

Ravi, her young neighbour who often carried finished shawls to the bus stand, came in just then with a sack of dyed wool. He caught the tail end of our conversation.

"Didi," he said, "you don't stop weaving just because the sun hides behind the clouds. You finish the shawl and dry it when the sun is out. Maybe your orders can work the same way?"

"That's exactly what I'm saying," I added. "Digital doesn't have to mean live internet every second. You can work offline, save your orders, stock lists, even pictures, and when you go to an area with a better network, everything will update automatically." You can also mention, 'Contact for discounts on bulk orders.'

Nisha leaned back and looked at me carefully. "So I keep typing into the phone, but nothing leaves until I say so?"

"Yes," I said. "Think of it like writing letters at home. You don't wait till you are standing at the post office counter to write them. You prepare them, and when the post office is open, you send them all at once."

Ravi laughed. "So the internet is the bus, and the orders are the passengers. The bus may be late, but the passengers are ready."

Nisha's brow softened, but her doubt hadn't left. "And what if the phone breaks before I reach the network?"

"You would have written those in your notebook anyway, and once your business scales, we can look at advanced options of backup in hard drives, etc. Currently, you don't need those. And let's keep the hope and don't consider the extreme cases for now, as to what happens if your notebook gets dry or lost."

Nisha thought for a moment and then said, "If I try this, we start small. I don't want the whole business shifting in one day."

We agreed. Step one would be:

1. Orders entered into an offline-friendly app on her phone, with photos stored alongside.

2. Stock list updated with colour codes: green for ready, yellow for reserved, red for sold.

3. A weekly Google Drive backup from mobile with access to a few people.

The first week was awkward. Nisha typed slowly, double-checking every entry. Once, she forgot to attach the photo of a shawl. Another time, Ravi labelled a sold item as "ready" and Nisha had to correct it.

But by the second week, the system started feeling like part of the day. The looms clicked, the tandoor warmed the room, and somewhere between winding wool and serving tea, Nisha would enter her orders without fuss.

The Festival Test

In October, the Kullu Dussehra filled the valley with music, colour, and tourists. One afternoon, a Delhi boutique owner walked in and spent nearly an hour choosing designs. She placed an order for twenty shawls. "Send me the pictures tonight so I can finalise the mix," she said, handing over her card.

By evening, the signal was gone. Not even a single bar. Nisha paced the workshop. "She will think I forgot her. Or worse, that I am unprofessional."

Ravi remained calm. "We already have the photos in the app. Give me your phone." He connected it to his laptop, copied the folder to a USB stick, and tucked it in his pocket.

"I'll take the morning bus to Kullu," he said. "There's a cybercafé near the bus stand. By the time you finish your tea tomorrow, she will have the pictures."

The next day, true to his word, the email was sent from town. By noon, the boutique owner replied: "Confirmed. Advance transferred."

When Ravi read out the message, Nisha laughed in relief. "So the internet can go wherever it wants, my orders will still travel."

Mini-Framework: Digital Steps Without Internet Dependence

Step	Action	Why It Works
1	Use offline-friendly apps for orders and inventory	Keeps work going without live internet
2	Store data and photos locally	Safe during outages
3	Maintain regular backups on Google Drive, a pen drive, or a hard drive.	Prevents total loss if the device is damaged
4	Sync during trips to better-signal areas	Reduces the stress of immediate connectivity
5	Train a helper to manage updates	Makes the system run even if the owner is busy or away

Reflection

Nisha's fear was not about technology. It was about the helplessness of watching opportunity vanish because she could not respond in time. By separating the act of working from the act of sending, she found freedom. She could weave, record, and prepare without waiting for a flickering signal.

Her shawls still carry the touch of her hands. Now, her business records are saved three times: once on her phone, another in Google Drive whenever she's online, and on a hard drive or a pen drive for offline access. She wanted to be sure, having lost many businesses due to unavailability.

Chapter 23: The Cost of a Seasonal Mindset

"The reasonable man adapts himself to the world; the unreasonable one persists in trying to adapt the world to himself. Therefore, all progress depends on the unreasonable man."

- *George Bernard Shaw*

The air in Mr Rao's small cashew processing unit in Visakhapatnam carried the faint, sweet scent of roasted nuts and the hum of a thousand stories. For decades, his family's business had operated in perfect tune with the land's rhythm. For Mr Rao, a man in his late fifties with calloused hands and a calm, knowing smile, the year was divided into two distinct parts: the feverish harvest season and the long, quiet off-season. For three to four months a year, his unit was a hive of activity. Cashew nuts arrived in sacks from local farms, the roasting ovens worked non-stop, and his team of workers meticulously shelled, graded, and packed the final product. The rest of the year was for managing existing stock, nurturing relationships, and preparing for the next harvest. It was a life of simple profit and predictable cycles.

I met him in his office; a tiny room filled with stacks of worn ledgers and the sweet aroma of jaggery from his morning tea. He looked up, his eyes holding the wisdom of a man who had seen too many harvests to be surprised by any. "They tell me to go digital," he said, gesturing vaguely toward the town. "My son keeps showing me apps for inventory and websites for selling. But I ask him, why? I work 4-5 months a year. Why should I digitise for the whole year? The cost of being digital for the whole year is pointless. It doesn't match my business. It doesn't make sense."

His apprehension was not a rejection of progress but a deeply held, logical belief that a solution built for a year-round, city-based enterprise would be a poor fit for his seasonal operation. He saw the digital world as a full-time, always-on commitment; a treadmill that never stopped, even when his business did. He was a master of his craft, and his system, built on trust, handshakes, and a leather-bound book, had worked flawlessly for decades. His biggest fear was that this new, "always-on" approach would be a costly and unnecessary burden that would force him to change the very essence of how he ran his life and business.

The Unseen Friction

The problem with Mr Rao's logic was that the world around him wasn't operating on his seasonal calendar anymore. The invisible friction, a quiet but relentless force, began to surface. His largest buyer, a wholesaler in Hyderabad, started to demand a weekly stock report via a messaging app. Mr Rao would have to call his son, who would then have to go to the locked shed, physically count the sacks, and send a message back. The process was slow and cumbersome, frustrating the buyer who wanted a real-time count.

More critically, a young farmer he had worked with for years, a man who grew the finest cashews, switched to a new buyer. When Mr Rao asked him why, the farmer explained, "The new buyer paid me immediately, with one click, using an app on my phone. They didn't have to wait for the banks to open. It was instant." The loyalty that had been built over the years was beginning to be eroded by the sheer convenience of a system that didn't stop for seasons.

The most painful incident, however, was a missed opportunity. A buyer from a boutique grocery chain in Chennai, having heard of his reputation for quality, called him in the off-season. "I need 500 kilos of premium cashews for a special order. Can you confirm stock and pricing now?" Mr Rao, who was on a brief vacation, had to say he would check when he got back. By the time he returned and found the information, the deal was gone. His seasonal mindset had cost him a year-round customer. He conceded with a sinking feeling that his business was no longer an island. The digital currents he had tried to avoid had found a way to reach him. His system, while perfect for his own rhythms, was increasingly out of sync with the broader market.

The Staggered Growth Plan: From Seasonal to Strategic

His son, Vivek, a software engineer who had recently returned to help with the family business, understood his father's apprehension completely. He knew a full-scale digital leap would be a disaster. So we proposed a staggered growth plan, a slow and deliberate adoption that respected the natural rhythm of the business and made the digital tools work for them, not the other way around. We called it "smart scaling."

Phase 1: The Harvest-Time Hack. The first step was to digitalise the immediate pain points of the busy season, not the whole business. Vivek introduced a simple, free-to-use digital ledger app. Instead of a paper book, all transactions, from buying from farmers to selling to buyers, were recorded on a tablet. This didn't change the process; it simply made it faster and more accurate. Mr Rao could now send a WhatsApp message with a snapshot of the ledger to his buyers, confirming stock instantly. The new system also automatically calculated totals and tracked payments, eliminating manual errors and late-night tallying. This was a direct, immediate, and visible benefit that didn't require any year-round work.

Phase 2: The Off-Season Build. The core of the plan was what we did during the eight quiet months. Instead of shutting down digitally, we used this time to build a low-maintenance, foundational digital presence. Vivek created a simple, one-page website. It didn't have an e-commerce function or a flashy interface. Its purpose was to tell their story. The website featured high-resolution photos of the cashew orchards, a brief history of their family business, and a gallery of their products with a simple "Contact us for pricing" button. During the off-season, Mr Rao and Vivek would post one or two pictures a week on social media platforms, showing the sun-drying process or the unique properties of their cashews. This was content-based marketing, not sales. This digital presence was like a digital brochure; it worked for them all year, telling their story and building a presence with almost zero effort and cost.

Phase 3: Strategic Expansion. Once we saw the value of the first two phases, we began to use the off-season more proactively. Mr Rao acknowledged he could use the time to nurture relationships with the people who had found them through their website. They launched a small-scale, direct-to-consumer model for local grocery stores in other cities, allowing them to take pre-orders for the next harvest. The digital infrastructure they had built was now a tool for extending their business beyond their physical location and their harvest-time window. The business was still seasonal in its operations, but it was now year-round in its reach and potential. The digital tools weren't a burden; they were a strategic lever, allowing them to work smarter, not harder.

The New Outlook: Digital as an Extension of Culture

The transformation in Mr Rao's mindset was profound. He now saw that his traditional values, the focus on quality, the personal relationships with farmers, and the rhythm of the seasons, were not opposed to digital tools; they were the very things that made his digital presence so compelling.

He learned that technology adoption isn't about a one-size-fits-all solution. It must be part of your culture, and in his case, that meant it had to be seasonal. A full-year digital commitment would have broken his business; a staggered, strategic plan made it stronger. He admitted that the cost of digitalising for the whole year was nothing compared to the opportunity cost of not being found, not being able to communicate instantly, and not being able to seize opportunities when they arose. His business was still rooted in the soil of Visakhapatnam, but its reputation and reach now extended to places he could never have imagined. The paper ledger was not replaced, but it was now supported by a digital system that gave him peace of mind and the agility to compete in a world that never truly sleeps.

Mini-Framework: Digital for the Micro-Enterprise

- **Start with the Pain Point:** Don't digitalise everything at once. Identify the one or two most frustrating, time-consuming parts of your business and find a simple, low-cost digital tool to solve just that.

- **Use the Quiet Time to Build:** Use your slow periods not as downtime, but as an opportunity to build a digital presence that requires minimal effort to maintain throughout the year. This could be a basic website, a social media profile, or a content plan.

- **Digitalise with a Purpose:** Your digital journey should be unique to your business. Don't copy a competitor's e-commerce store if you have no plans to be an e-commerce business. Use technology to amplify your unique value proposition, not to fit a mould.

- **Measure with Your Own Metrics:** The return on investment for a micro-enterprise isn't just in sales. It's in time saved, stress reduced, better relationships, and access to opportunities that were previously out of reach.

Reflection

Mr Rao's journey is a powerful case study for any micro-enterprise owner who fears the digital world. His initial apprehension was perfectly logical; a full-scale digital makeover for a seasonal business is a recipe for failure. The key was to understand that technology is a tool, and its effectiveness depends entirely on how it is wielded. By adopting a staggered, culturally relevant approach, he not only survived but also found a way to honour his traditions while securing his future. He didn't have to give up his off-season rest; he learned to use it to his strategic advantage. His business, once defined by its seasonal nature, was now defined by its resilience and its thoughtful approach to growth.

Chapter 24: Beyond the Paper Slip

"The biggest challenge in business is not competition, it is complacency."

— Azim Premji

Varanasi wakes early, but the wholesale markets wake up even earlier. By the time the temple bells ring at dawn, Godowlia's narrow lanes are alive with the clatter of shutters, the grunts of porters dragging sacks of rice and sugar, and the horns of small trucks reversing into impossible spaces. The smells are layered: jaggery from a sweet shop, turmeric dust from a spice sack, and the faint smoke curling out of a tea stall that has been serving since first light.

In the middle of this commotion stood Ashok Mittal's kirana wholesale shop. From outside, it looked like any other: a faded signboard, a counter at the front, and sacks piled high. Inside, every inch was filled with stock, yet there was just enough room for the three people who kept it alive.

Ashok sat at the front desk, pen scratching across the pages of a thick ledger. Around him were carbon-copy books, bundles of invoices tied with string, and slips tucked into corners of the counter. His son Sumit moved in and out of the storeroom, balancing cartons on his shoulder. A young helper counted biscuits into neat piles on the floor.

"Everyone these days talks about computers, digital invoices, GST software," Ashok said before I could ask anything. "But what use is that here? My clients still want paper invoices. They want something they can hold, something to file away and keep. They do not care for emails or PDFs. So why should I waste money on printers and apps when paper already works?"

He pulled out a bundle of slips tied with twine and spread them across the counter like a deck of cards. "See these. Every transaction is here. My clients come back even after years with these in hand and say, Mittal ji, you wrote this yourself. How can I deny it? They trust paper. Maybe in Delhi, people have moved to digital. Here, a slip is the only proof that matters."

The helper on the floor looked up. "But, sir, sometimes slips get misplaced. Then customers argue, and we lose time."

Ashok waved him off. "That happens in every business. My customers know me."

From the back, Sumit came forward. "Bauji, last Diwali we lost thirty thousand rupees because of missing slips and delayed payments. We only realised it when I checked the accounts weeks later. If we had proper records, we could have avoided that."

Ashok frowned. "You are young. You do not understand this market. Our clients are old-school. They do not want digital. They want their slips."

As if on cue, a small shopkeeper walked in, envelope in hand. He greeted Ashok and pulled out a crumpled paper slip.

"Last month I bought twenty bags of rice," he said firmly. "I paid cash. But your man is saying I still owe for ten bags. Here is the slip."

Ashok flipped through his ledger and produced another slip. He showed only ten bags.

"So which is correct?" the customer demanded. "I cannot pay twice."

Ashok asked the helper. The boy stammered, "I do not remember, Bauji. That day was too busy."

The customer muttered angrily and left dissatisfied. Ashok closed the ledger with a sigh. "This is the headache of paper. But customers demand it."

That evening, over chai outside, Sumit spoke again. "Bauji, nobody is asking you to stop giving slips. Customers will always get paper. But we can take a photo of each slip and keep it in a WhatsApp folder. That way, if one is lost, we still have proof. No cost, no change for the customer."

Ashok stayed silent, stirring his chai, unwilling to admit but clearly thinking.

Back at the desk, I asked for his phone. I showed him how a slip photo could be saved in a folder. "Paper for them, digital copy for you. One lock can break, two keep you safe."

He nodded slowly. "Customers will not accept digital alone."

"Then do not give it alone," Sumit said. "Give both."

When I returned during the Diwali rush, the shop was overflowing with sacks of sugar and cartons of dry fruits. Helpers ran in and out, voices shouting over each other.

A dispute broke out. A trader claimed he had ordered thirty cartons of biscuits, but Ashok's slip showed twenty. Ashok grew irritated as he shuffled papers. Before the argument grew louder, Sumit pulled out his phone.

"Here is the photo of the slip," he said. "It shows thirty ordered, twenty delivered, ten pending."

The trader looked at both the paper and the phone. He agreed to wait for the balance to be paid. The dispute ended, not with magic, but with both parties supporting each other's records.

Ashok leaned back, astonished. "If we had relied only on slips, we would have wasted an hour today."

Sumit proposed a new routine. "At closing time, we spend ten minutes entering orders into a simple app. Not during rush, only after hours. Customers still get slips. We still take photos. But now we also have a clean record for ourselves."

Ashok tested it for a month. Nothing changed for customers — they still walked away with their slips. However, for the shop, parallel records meant disputes ended more quickly and payments were tracked more effectively. Even the helper was relieved: "Now we do not panic when a slip is missing. We know a copy is safe."

Ashok finally admitted, "Paper comforts the customer. Digital protects the business. Both can live together."

Mini-Framework: From Paper to Digital in Wholesale

1. Keep slips for customer trust. Respect habits, do not force change.

2. Take phone photos of every slip. Free, instant, and effective backup.

3. Do end-of-day digital entry. Ten minutes is enough to record daily totals in a free app.

4. Use WhatsApp for repeat buyers. Share invoices directly so both sides have copies.

5. Review seasonally. Compare disputes and losses before and after. Let ROI guide expansion.

Reflection

For years, Ashok Mittal believed digital had no place in his wholesale shop because customers demanded paper. But the cost of lost slips and disputes was eating into profit. The experiment with photos and end-of-day entries showed him a new way. Digital was not about replacing paper. It was about adding a safety net.

The paper gave customers comfort. Digital gave the business protection. Together, they reduced disputes, saved money, and prepared the shop for compliance that would soon become mandatory. ROI came not as sudden profit but as fewer losses and more control.

For every small business in traditional markets, the lesson is clear. You do not need to abandon the habits your customer's trust. But you also cannot afford to ignore the protection digital offers. The smartest path is not paper or digital. It is both, side by side.

Chapter 25: Don't Just Run a Business. Build One That Runs Without You

"Don't automate chaos. Organise first, then digitalise."

- *Adapted from Bill Gates*

When I stepped into the narrow by-lane of Barshi in Maharashtra, I wasn't sure what to expect. Locals pointed me toward a small grocery and distribution setup tucked between a paan shop and a tyre repair stall. There was no signboard, but I didn't need one. I could hear the voice before I saw the shop.

"Bhai, tell Rakesh that his Dabur consignment is already packed! And ask Dinesh to wait, I'll give him the cheque myself!"

That was Ramesh Solanki, the owner, the accountant, the stockist, the manager, and, if needed, the tempo driver too. By the time I reached the front counter, he had already spoken to three suppliers, adjusted one invoice, and passed a biscuit packet to a regular customer who didn't need to say a word. Everything about him was fast, fluid, and fiercely precise.

"Sit," he said, wiping his forehead with a towel slung over his shoulder. "But don't start with your tech gyaan. I know what I'm doing. Ask me anything about my business, stock, sales, or customer history. I'll answer faster than your so-called system." Additionally, should I do my core work or fill in details on a mobile app to share my data, and if so, why and with whom?

I smiled because this wasn't ego. It was a direct, lived experience and utility-based approach.

A Shop That Breathes Its Owner

The shop was small, but alive. Every corner had a purpose. Boxes were stacked in a pattern only Rameshbhai understood. He could spot a mislabelled carton from ten feet away. "That Surf packet belongs in the third row. This one's the school order, don't mix it," he told his assistant while still checking accounts on his phone.

I followed him around for an hour. No chair. No pause. Just Rameshbhai in motion. He answered calls, greeted customers by name, cracked jokes with suppliers, and never once opened a ledger.

"You see now?" he said, catching his breath. "Why do I need software when my brain works like one?"

I didn't argue. But I also disagreed.

What Happens When the Machine Sleeps?

Later, while sipping tea on a bench outside, I asked, "What happens when you're not here?"

He raised an eyebrow. "Meaning?"

"What if you're unwell? Or need to travel suddenly? Who runs the shop?"

"My brother helps. Sometimes my daughter comes in, too."

"And do they know the system?"

He was quiet for a moment. "No one can run it like I do."

"That's true," I said. "But shouldn't they at least be able to run it at all?"

He sipped his tea slowly. "So you're saying, forget fast, I need to make it replicable?"

"Exactly," I said. "You're not just running a shop. You're holding a legacy. Don't let it disappear if you're not around for a day."

Making the Invisible Visible

The next morning, I returned. No laptop. No app demos. Just a notepad and a sketch pen.

We stood by the counter. "Let's write down just one thing today," I said. "How do you check the daily stock?"

He dictated. I wrote. His daughter, Rutuja, watched quietly. When we finished, she took a photo of the sheet and typed it out on her phone.

That evening, she created a colour-coded chart in Google Sheets and printed it out to post on the counter.

"No harm in trying," she said. "At least when Baba's not here, I won't panic."

Rameshbhai didn't say much. But the next morning, he pointed to the chart when his helper asked about the stock of toothpaste.

Digital Doesn't Mean Start with Digital, Organise First.

We didn't buy software. We didn't install CCTV. We have just begun documenting the existing knowledge.

In other parts of India, similar shifts are happening quietly. A couple in Coimbatore uses WhatsApp voice notes to record the day's sales after closing, and an Artificial Intelligence (AI) app extracts the information from the voice note, summarises the sale, and predicts the next steps for the next day.

It's not about replacing the human system. It's about supporting it.

Building a Digital-First Habit Without Losing Your Core

What You Already Do Well	Simple Digital Support	What It Adds
You remember all your stock	Create a shared checklist on paper or phone	Makes business less dependent on one person
You know your customers deeply	Use WhatsApp broadcast or any such tool for updates	Helps you stay connected even if you're away
You manage orders verbally	Record them with voice notes with any app	Prevents errors and helps juniors follow
You rely on routines	Visual cues (charts, printouts) in the shop	Allows smoother handover and better planning

Reflection

Rameshbhai is not just a shopkeeper; he's a living system, a memory bank, and a decision-making engine. But even he began to realise that true strength isn't just in knowing everything, it's in making that knowledge usable by others.

Going digital didn't mean replacing him. It meant protecting his way of working by making it accessible, even when he was absent. That's the essence of a digital-first mindset: not putting technology above people, but using technology to empower people when they need it most.

Chapter 26: Trust Is Built on Chai, Not Clicks

"The art challenges the technology, and the technology inspires the art."

— John Lasseter

Shillong wakes to light rain and early traffic. By eight, shutters lift in Police Bazaar and handcarts move through the side lanes. Inside a ground-floor unit called Pinehill Cane Works, bundles of rattan stand against one wall and a hand press clicks in a steady rhythm. A red register lies open on a steel table.

Marcia Dkhar owns the unit. Her cousin Benedict manages cutting and tying. Her niece Risa, a college student, helps with messages after class. They make stools, café chairs, and woven lampshades for shops in Guwahati, Silchar, and Agartala.

I asked Marcia how she prefers to take orders.

"Face to face," she said and poured tea. "We meet, agree, and shake hands. Trust starts at this table. Not on a screen."

Risa waited and then spoke.

"Aunty, buyers move fast on the phone now. They want a clear photo and a one-line confirmation. If we reply late, they place the order elsewhere."

Benedict pointed to the register. Three orders were open. One payment was already ten days late.

"We lost a café in Beltola last week," he said. "They chose a vendor who sent a morning photo and closed in ten minutes."

Marcia looked at the page for a long moment.

"So we lost on speed," she said. "Not on finish."

The hesitation

"Digital is noisy," Marcia said. "If I sit with the phone, who will check sizes or tighten a loose weave. Work has to move."

I requested a one-week trial with two conditions. The register will remain the final book. No group chats and no price negotiation on messages. She agreed.

A small trial that fits the room

Risa cleared one table near the door for photos. She taped a white sheet to the wall and kept a marker and a measuring tape on the table.

She proposed two changes.

First change. Two fixed messages each day.

At eight forty-five, she would send one photo and a single line. For example, Stools S1 and café chairs C2 are ready, counts and dispatch day. At 4:15, she would send a second short note for next-day preorders. These messages would go to a broadcast list of regular buyers. There would be no group chat.

Second change. A quick call for significant asks.

If a buyer asked for more than a set quantity, Risa would call within ten minutes to repeat the item, count, rate, and dispatch day. She would write the call time in the register on that buyer's row.

Marcia agreed because neither step slowed the floor, and the register still stayed in charge.

The first morning message went out on time. Replies appeared within minutes. A Guwahati décor store booked twenty stools S1. A Silchar boutique wanted ten lampshades L3. A café in Khanapara asked for a close-up of a joint. Risa called the Guwahati store, repeated the numbers, and wrote the call time in the register. She sent the joint photo and received a clear yes.

Marcia watched the table and said one sentence that mattered.

"This is visibility," she said. "Not a new kind of work."

Noise and how to handle it

Speed brought noise. A new customer was offered at a very low price with thirty days of credit. Risa sent a one-line reply that they had written and pinned above the desk. Rates as per the catalogue. Credit by relationship only. Token or bank credit before dispatch.

The new client went quiet. Two regular buyers asked for minor corrections. One wanted five more stools. One wanted a size change from eighteen inches to twenty. Both corrections arrived before cutting, so no material was wasted.

"Cut to count," Marcia told Benedict. "No extra today."

Guardrails that kept order

By the end of the week, they wrote three rules on a sheet and taped it above the register.

The register is the master.

Messages support speed and proof. Every commitment is recorded in the register with the buyer's initials, item code, quantity, rate, dispatch date, and call time for large orders.

One dispatch photo per order.

Before the tempo leaves, Risa takes one photo with labels visible and a slip with the date inside the top carton. She sends it to the buyer. Late-night calls are reduced.

Quiet hours are protected.

Replies go out at noon and at eight in the evening. After hours, the auto reply says, Thank you. We will confirm at eight forty-five.

What changed in three weeks

The changes were visible on the shop floor.

Morning orders arrived before cutting. The unit cut fewer extra strips. Wastage from wrong sizes and overcutting has been reduced. Two buyers who used to call three times on dispatch day stopped calling because the dispatch photo answered most questions. One buyer who often delayed payment sent a bank transfer after receiving the dispatch photo. Cash handling at day's end became easier.

Not everything went well. A new buyer showed a false payment screenshot at pickup. Marcia kept the carton back and asked to see the credit in the bank app. The buyer returned the next day and paid. Risa saved the number in a watch list.

Meetings still matter

Old buyers still wanted to meet. Marcia visited a Guwahati shop owned by Anindita Paul. The family has been in home décor for years.

"Your morning note helps our team plan," Anindita said. "When you change a joint, bring two samples. We decide faster when we hold the piece."

Marcia agreed.

"The phone will not replace the bench," she said. "It will reduce unclear calls."

On the drive back, she repeated the line she began with.

"Chai for decisions. Phone for speed."

Small systems that stayed

They wrote product codes that match how the floor speaks. S1 and S2 for two stool designs. C2 for the café chair. L3 for lampshades. The same codes appear on cartons, in messages, and in the register. Counting errors fell because everyone read the same two letters and one number.

They defined one recovery step when a defect is reported. If a buyer sends a photo of a loose tie, Risa logs it against the dispatch entry. Benedict checks that the weaving step is on the next batch. This prevented repeats within the same week.

They added a Saturday review. The register is matched to photos and bank credits. Any mismatch is fixed that day. The review now takes thirty minutes.

Mini Framework: Keep the chai, add the clicks

- Send a single morning note about your product: one clear photo and one line with ready items, counts, and a dispatch window.

167

- Confirm large orders over the phone. After any large message, make a short call to repeat the item, count, rate, and dispatch.

- Use the codes the floor already uses. Keep codes short and put them on cartons, messages, and in the register.

- Send dispatch proof. One photo with labels visible and a dated slip inside the top carton ends most avoidable doubts.

- Protect quiet hours. Fix two reply windows. Use a polite auto reply after hours.

- Keep the register as the final book until you become comfortable with a completely digital system. Let messages support speed and proof, not replace control.

- Review once a week. Match register lines, photos, and bank credits. Close gaps the same day.

Reflection

This unit did not replace meetings with messages. It added simple visibility so buyers could plan and production could cut to real numbers. Trust was still formed across the table. Messages reduced distance and doubt. The register kept authority. The outcome was fewer surprises, less waste, and steadier collections. The phone remains noisy at times. Routine keeps that noise under control.

Marcia still says that trust is built on tea at the table. She now adds that a clear morning note earns the right to pour that tea.

Chapter 27: Digitally Enabled or Overwhelmed?

"The future is already here; it's just not evenly distributed."

– William Gibson

It was late afternoon in Gaya, Bihar. The bazaar was alive with its usual rhythm, a rhythm made of noise, smells, and movement. Vegetable carts lined up in a row, their owners calling out prices in sharp voices. Children ran across the road as auto rickshaws honked without pause. From a corner stall came the smell of fried pakoras mixed with the dust rising from the road. It was the kind of atmosphere where nothing seemed calm, but everything somehow functioned.

In the middle of this bazaar stood Saraswati Agro and General Store, painted a bright but fading blue. Sacks of fertiliser, seed packets, tins of oil, and even packets of biscuits were stacked at the entrance. Inside, the narrow space was filled to the roof. Behind the counter sat Ramesh Prasad, a man in his early fifties with a careful moustache and eyes that looked both proud and tired. He waved me in warmly.

"You have come to talk about digital," he said even before I sat down. "Let me tell you first, we are already digital. I put my stock updates on WhatsApp and Facebook. Farmers message me directly. For billing, I have accounting software on my computer. It prints invoices and calculates GST. What else is there? We are already ahead of many in this town."

He pushed his phone across the counter. I scrolled through his gallery. It was filled with pictures of seed packets and fertiliser bags, each with captions written in Hindi. Beneath the images were short comments. Rate. Delivery. Available today. The posts were working.

"You see," he said, leaning back. "My father had to wait for word of mouth. I can reach the whole village with one click. Tell me, is that not digital?"

I asked gently, "Ramesh ji, this is the use of digital tools. But do you think your business overall is integrated and is helping you to take the next business decision for growth and compliance?"

He frowned. "What difference is there. Digital is digital."

At that moment, his son, Aman, walked in, carrying two glasses of chai. He laughed softly, clearly having heard the conversation many times before.

"Papaji thinks digital means only Facebook and invoices," he whispered to me, then spoke louder. "Papaji, last season we lost almost fifteen thousand rupees in delayed collections. Your software made invoices, yes, but it did not tell us who was late. By the time we realised, months had passed."

Ramesh looked defensive. "That happens in every business. We check the register when we have time."

I said, "That is not digital-first. Digital-first means the system tells you who is late, how many days have passed, and when to follow up. It should remind us of our language. We should not have to dig through registers."

As if to underscore the point, a farmer walked in carrying a folded piece of paper. "Bhaiya, last month I bought fertiliser bags. I paid cash, but your helper says it is not in the system. Here is the slip."

Ramesh opened his ledger, searched his billing software, and grew restless. The entry was missing. The farmer's voice grew firmer.

I stepped forward quickly. "Chacha, from today, we will note your name in the new app. We can speak into the phone in Hindi, and it will record your purchase instantly. Next time, there will be no confusion." I pressed the microphone button and spoke in a clear voice. "Ravi Kumar, ten bags of fertiliser, paid in cash." The words appeared on the screen. Beneath it was a line showing payment status as settled.

The farmer nodded slowly. "If you keep my name like this, then there will be no fight. At least you will have proof."

Ramesh watched in silence. He had never seen something so simple that even he could use it without needing to type.

I replied, "Digital is not just for showing. It is for knowing. If a trader does not know who has paid and who is delaying, then what use is his software?"

Another man asked curiously, "But these new apps, will they not cost a lot. Will they bring sales?"

I explained, "Some are free or very cheap. And the return is not just in sales, but also in savings. It is at peace of mind. When you know which customer is delaying and which seed sells the most during the rabi season, you can make better decisions. That is the real return."

The next morning, I travelled a few kilometres out of town to visit a poultry farm run by Shanti Devi. She was in her forties, standing in the yard with a bamboo basket of grain. Hundreds of hens clucked loudly around her. She spread the feed with practised rhythm."We are already digital," she said with a smile. "We take orders on WhatsApp. Restaurants pay us on UPI. That is enough."

Her daughter, a college student, interrupted. "Amma, every week we buy feed, pay for electricity, and sell eggs. We write all this in three notebooks. We never know if the farm is making a profit or a loss. Sometimes the hens eat more, sometimes less. If we had an app that shows costs and sales in one place, we could clearly see our profit. It even shows how demand rises during festival time. Then we can plan stock properly."

Shanti Devi paused. "I thought WhatsApp was enough. But maybe I was wrong. Last Diwali, we sold everything fast, but we still felt short of money. We never knew why."

Her daughter replied, "Because we did not track costs against sales. If we had, we would know if the farm is growing or shrinking."

A neighbour who also kept poultry added, "My son uses one such app. He speaks in Bhojpuri, and it records everything. Last month, he showed me a report that stated winter feed consumption is higher, so we must save extra money for that season. I never thought of that. Now I feel more secure."

Shanti Devi listened carefully. She realised digital-first was not about orders alone. It was about clarity.

In Muzaffarpur, I met Arvind Agarwal, who ran a medium-sized cold storage. The building stood at the edge of the highway, walls painted white, a large steel gate at the front. Trucks came and went, unloading potatoes, onions, and cauliflower.

Inside, Arvind sat in an office stacked with files. "We have ERP software. But my staff says it is complicated. So we use it only for invoices. For stock, we rely on registers. We estimate which crops sell more based on our experience and market research. My father also guessed. That is enough."

He pulled out a register filled with scribbles. His nephew, standing nearby, smiled politely and opened his phone. On the screen was a dashboard created from simple voice entries made by workers.

"Look, Chacha Ji," he said. "This shows which crops sold better in which month. It shows which buyers delayed payment and the duration of the delay. It even shows patterns. Onions peak in July. Potatoes peak in October. You never noticed these details."

Arvind looked closer. "This is clear. Earlier, we lost stock because the humidity rose, and no one noticed. Here, the graph shows it. We can plan for it. One season of reduced loss has already covered the cost of this app."

For the first time, he saw digital not as a burden but as a guide.

Back in Gaya, I patiently explained the situation to Ramesh. "Digital-first does not mean giving up your habits. You can still post on WhatsApp and keep your register. However, digital-first means asking at each step, 'Can digital make this better and more efficient?' To find out who has not paid, open the app. It tells you who is late and by how many days. If you want to know which seeds sold the most in the last season, the app displays this information. It is like having a helper who never forgets."

Ramesh sipped his chai slowly. The young helper who had been listening quietly spoke up. "Bhaiya, this will also make my work easier. No more arguments with customers when slips go missing. I can show proof quickly."

Ramesh nodded. He was not ready to abandon paper, but he admitted that digital-first meant more than just posting online. It was managing the unseen parts of the business with the same care as the visible ones.

Mini-Framework: From Digital Adoption to Digital-First

1. Continue using social media for visibility, but remember that it is only a shop window.

2. Record sales and payments through mobile apps that allow voice entry in the local language.

3. Use dashboards that clearly display delayed payments, seasonal demand, and top-selling items. Apps now use Artificial Intelligence (AI) to help you predict based on your interactions and business profile.

4. Start with one problem area. If payment delays are most concerning, start with reminders. If wastage is high, start with stock tracking. Using AI will also help you get business insights and suggestions. Consider a generic consultant for advice.

5. Review results at the end of each season. Measure not just sales but time saved and disputes avoided.

Reflection

For Ramesh in Gaya, digital meant WhatsApp and Facebook posts, as well as accounting software. For Shanti Devi, it meant UPI and group orders. For Arvind, it meant billing through ERP. Each thought they were already digital. But disputes, delays, and wastage showed otherwise.

The shift occurred when they began to view digital as the primary lens, not the last step. Ramesh learned that speaking into a phone in Hindi could secure every order. Shanti Devi realised that a dashboard could display both costs and profits, revealing why money seemed scarce even in a good season. Arvind discovered that seasonal patterns, invisible to the naked eye, were hidden in his own data.

Digital-first does not mean abandoning trust, paper, or relationships. It means strengthening them with clarity. It does not erase the chai with farmers or bargaining in the mandi. It ensures those conversations are backed by facts rather than memory. ROI is not only about increasing sales. It is also about reducing mistakes, making more accurate forecasts, and gaining confidence in every decision.

Section 4: Guidance, Support & Enablers

Once MSMEs are convinced about *why* digital matters, the next hurdle is *how* to begin. The fear of choosing the wrong consultant, wasting money on bad agencies, or convincing staff and suppliers can stall progress. This section provides clarity: how to pick the right partners, how to start small, and how to bring others in your ecosystem along for the ride. It's about turning confusion into action with the right support systems.

Chapter 28: Before the Tech, Find the Trust

"If you want to go fast, go alone. If you want to go far, go together."

— African Proverb

It was a cool, overcast morning when I arrived at the outer industrial belt of Aurangabad. Tall chimneys stood silent in the background, while forklifts rumbled across wide lanes of factory sheds. I had come to visit RPK Precision Tools. This medium-sized enterprise had quietly built a reputation for supplying high-quality customised tool heads and jigs for some of India's leading automotive and aerospace vendors.

The owner, Mr. Rajeev Kumar, was waiting in his office on the second floor. Soft-spoken, dressed in a grey half-sleeved shirt with his phone turned upside down on the table, he had the posture of someone who listens more than he speaks.

We exchanged greetings, and over tea, I asked him what made him hesitant about full-scale digital adoption.

He smiled politely. "We get this question often. People say, 'Why don't you have ERP? Why don't you digitalise your dispatches and vendor records?' My answer is simple: Who will guide us? And who will make sure it doesn't collapse halfway?"

He gestured toward the factory floor. "We're not against tech. But we can't afford disruptions. One error in the tool measurement halts our shipment to Bangalore. So we ask again: who is there to handhold us through this?"

Beyond Cost: The Real Barrier Is Isolation

Kumar ji wasn't worried about the lakhs it might take to onboard a digital platform. His hesitation was rooted in uncertainty.

"We have sixty-five workers, four quality inspectors, and seven CNC machines. But no one can lead a tech transition internally. Even if we bring in a vendor, who will maintain it later?"

That's when I told him about an industrial cluster in Coimbatore where textile firms were facing a similar challenge. Instead of jumping into complete ERP suites, they began with digitising just their loom performance metrics. A local MSME advisory NGO collaborated with them to develop a straightforward dashboard. One young woman from the unit was trained to handle it, and she slowly trained others. It began as a pilot and, over time, became standard.

"Where do you find such support?" he asked. "Everyone who comes to us is either trying to sell something or overpromises."

Support Exists, If You Know Where to Look

I shared with him the lesser-known yet impactful support channels we often overlook:

- MSME chambers and state-run business facilitation centres in Tamil Nadu, Gujarat, and Assam

- Sector-specific consultants with hands-on industry experience

- Local engineering colleges and rural polytechnic institutes are running digital internship programs

178

- Vendor associations that co-fund group training for clusters

- Government schemes offering subsidised pilots and shared services

"Start small," I said. "Even a leather exporter in Kanpur I know began with digitising just her packaging line with help from a government-backed tech hub."

He leaned in, thoughtfully. "Let's say I start with machine calibration monitoring. Who helps us decide what to choose?"

"Speak to your peers," I said. "A packaging unit in Hyderabad did just that. They consulted with three similar-sized units nearby before selecting a system. Ask for trial access. Then, make someone on your team the champion."

Curiosity, Quietly Turning Into Confidence

Over the next month, Kumar ji reached out a few times. The first call was cautious. A vendor had offered a ready-made package with flashy dashboards.

"Can ERP be implemented in one week?" he asked.

I smiled. "If it sounds too fast, it usually skips the real work."

Later, he messaged again. This time with a list: "One quote comes with no after-sales support. There is no plan in place for staff training. How do I choose?"

It was clear he was evaluating, not just exploring.

He consulted three vendors and two consultants. One candidate was from Pune, with good technical skills but no manufacturing background. Another was a firm based in Chennai, run by an ex-factory head who had supported clusters in the SIDCO belt. Their team focused on gradual integration and field-tested implementation.

The third consultant was based in Nashik and had experience with mid-size tooling vendors. He came recommended through Kumar ji's industry association.

Eventually, Kumar ji chose the Chennai-based consultant, not because of a glossy proposal, but for the clear three-phase rollout and structured handholding. The pilot would focus only on the quality control dashboard. A junior engineer from Kumar ji's team, a 24-year-old who had grown up in a nearby city, was trained to lead it.

Two months later, Kumar ji sent me an update. "We caught a measurement variance before it became a defective batch. This real-time QC view is a game-changer."

Then he added, "I was never afraid of digital. I was afraid of not knowing where to begin."

A Wider Pattern

Across the country, I've seen a common trend. From women-led agri-processing units in Assam to solar assembly workshops in Rajasthan, or even a bakery in Goa that digitalises its raw material tracker, most don't fear technology. They fear being left unsupported. Once they find the right nudge, they embrace it, one step at a time.

Mr. Kumar didn't revolutionise his business overnight. He researched. He asked. He listened. And most importantly, he built a support system first. That made the rest possible.

How to Find the Right Support to Go Digital

Challenge	What to Explore	Why It Helps
Unsure where to start	Local MSME chambers, Govt facilitation centres, peer clusters	Step-by-step guidance in your language
Fear of being unsupported	Field-tested consultants with real-world factory experience	Stay involved after rollout, not just setup
No digital expertise in the team	Identify 2-3 capable employees and upskill them progressively	Builds internal ownership and adaptability
Concern about cost and return	Look into pilot programs, co-funded initiatives, and vendor training schemes	Let you test before committing heavy budgets
Want honest advice	Talk to peers across regions and sizes	Learns from mistakes others have already made

Reflection

Mr. Kumar didn't go all in. He didn't buy a full-suite transformation tool or restructure his floor. He reframed the question: not "What will this cost me?" but "Who will walk this path with me?"

That single shift turned a daunting idea into a guided process. And that's when change truly begins.

Chapter 29: Hands on the Mill, Eyes on the Map

"The best teachers are those who show you where to look, but don't tell you what to see."

- *Alexandra K. Trenfor*

By nine, the courtyard of Malabar Organics had filled with the colour and smell of work. Cardamom pods are dried on bamboo trays. A heap of sun-warmed peppercorns crackled under a worker's palm. Inside the small processing shed, a grinder whirred, sending a clean ribbon of turmeric powder into a steel drum. The air carried the steam from a kettle and the sweet scent of cloves.

Anitha Menon waved me toward a bench near the doorway. She ran the unit with her younger brother, Sreejith. Their parents had sold bulk spices to traders for years. Anitha wanted to sell branded packets to stores in Kochi and Bengaluru. The plan sounded simple when she said it out loud. It did not feel simple on the floor.

"Can you just run the digital part for us?" she asked, pouring tea. "Set it up, talk to customers online, handle the website, software, the listings, all of it. We will look after quality and production. And we will pay from whatever we save or earn extra because of that digital effort."

I did not answer immediately. The grinder stopped. Someone tied off a bag with a quick pull of twine.

"Tell me what happened the last time you tried for help from outside," I said.

She smiled without humour. "You will like this story."

Three months earlier, a consultant had walked in with glossy samples and a fast tongue. He promised a store website within two weeks, online marketplace listings within a month, and a specific sales target for the first festival season. His proposal said he would manage everything. The words sounded like comfort to Anitha, who was already juggling purchase, roasting, grinding, packaging, and dispatch.

"He told me not to worry about small things," she said. "He would open all the accounts for us. Set the passwords. Post the photos. Manage the ads. We just had to send packets on time."

At first, it felt like progress. A logo appeared. A page went live. Two small stores called. Then the cracks showed. Customers wrote to an email address controlled by the consultant. Marketplace messages were answered late because only his team could see them. The first big order from a Kochi supermarket chain arrived without batch numbers recorded. The consultant had uploaded product pages without linking them to the traceability sheet that Anitha kept on paper. During a surprise inspection, the store requested proof of origin for each batch. No one could find it online. The goods were returned.

Sreejith entered the office carrying a stack of new sacks. "That week was terrible," he said. "We were not sure what had shipped. The consultant kept saying he had it under control. We did not even own the website password."

Anitha opened a drawer and pulled out a thin folder. "Here is the worst part. When we asked for access, he said it would be better if he kept it. He used words like optimisation and proprietary settings.

183

It sounded like we were children being allowed to watch our own shop from the window."

They ended the contract. It took ten days to recover their accounts and reset everything.

"So you want me to run it for you," I said. "Do you want to repeat the same mistake with a different face?"

She stirred her tea. "I do not want that. I want to ship on time, keep accurate records, and respond to customers promptly. But I cannot spend my day inside screens."

"Then do not hire a replacement owner," I said. "Hire a guide who builds your people. A good consultant should leave you stronger, not more dependent."

Sreejith leaned against the doorframe. "What would that look like here?"

"It begins on the floor," I said. "Not in a laptop. Let me watch one full batch today. No meetings outside. No slides. I want to see how information moves in this shed."

Walking the line

We walked with a fresh batch of pepper from the receipt to the dispatch. Anitha showed me the weighing table, the roasting drum, the grinder, the sifter, and the packing bench. She spoke in the rhythm of someone who has counted losses and learned from them.

"We record incoming lots on paper," she said. "Roast time is written in a notebook near the drum. Batch numbers are stamped at the packing table. Dispatch slips are filed by date."

"Who checks that the batch number on the packet is the same one on the dispatch slip?" I asked.

"Most days I do," she said. "If I am out meeting a buyer, Sreejith does it."

"Where do you keep the notebook entries once the day ends?"

"In a steel cupboard," she said, tapping it with the side of her hand.

We stood for a minute listening to the low rumble of the grinder starting again. A worker lifted a tray, and the smell of warm pepper filled the shed.

"This is where a trainer earns their fee," I said. "Not by taking over your work. By drawing a thin line from this pile of pepper to the receipt in a store, and making sure anyone on your team can follow that line."

We agreed on a one-month engagement with two conditions. First, every account, password, and dashboard would be created in Anitha's name. Second, any process introduced must be teachable to three people on her team within a week.

We began with a floor audit. Anitha's team walked me through one pepper batch from farm gate to sealed packet. Together, we built a simple map on a whiteboard. Six boxes. Receive, roast, grind, sift, pack, dispatch. Under each box, we wrote the exact paper document that already existed. Then we added a thin digital layer that did not disturb the habit. For receiving, a two-column entry in a shared sheet. For roasting, a picture of the drum panel with time and temperature. For packing, use a small sticker with a printed batch code and scan it with a phone camera to mark completion. For dispatch, a pick list that matched the batch codes.

Nothing fancy. No new jargon. We pinned the map to the wall next to the sifter.

In the afternoons, I sat with three people Anitha picked as champions. Radha from packing. Faizal from roasting. A young

185

accountant named Dileep had just joined. We practised until each could do the other's task. By the fourth day, Radha could scan a batch code, check the pick list, and catch a mismatch before it left the shed. She saw one that week. The returned goods from Kochi still stung. Everyone noticed when she held up the wrong label and said, with a slight smile, "Not this one."

The stress test

Onam orders landed like a wave. A supermarket in Kochi placed a rush order for six varieties, all of which had new packaging that the store had approved only a day earlier. Two small organic stores in Thrissur added medium packs at the last minute. The old Anitha would have moved from station to station, correcting, checking, and shouting over the hum of machines. That morning, she stood at the doorway and watched.

Dileep called out the incoming lots and wrote them on the shared sheet. Faizal updated roast times with a quick photo of the drum panel. Radha scanned batch stickers at the packing bench and matched them to the pick list. When the truck arrived, Sreejith read out each carton code and ticked it off against the dispatch list. Anitha took two calls from buyers and answered both without leaving the door. She had the list on her phone. She could see what had cleared and what was still at the bench.

There were small mistakes. A tray of turmeric reached the packing table without a sticker. Radha stopped it, fixed it, and put it back in line. A carton for Thrissur was mistakenly labelled as Kochi. The code scan caught it. No one raised their voice. The work kept moving.

By evening, the truck left with every carton listed, each tied to a batch code that could be traced back to a sack on the receiving mat. Anitha closed the metal door and leaned against it for a second.

"This is the first Onam I have not gone home with a headache," she said.

What changed?

At the end of the month, we met in the small office. No presentation. Just the floor map now smudged with fingerprints and the whiteboard crowded with small notes. Anitha ticked off the list.

"We own every account," she said. "We can change a password without asking anyone. Three people can follow a batch from entry to dispatch. Our website logins are in my drawer and in the safe. The store emails come to our inbox. Radha replies to the marketplace messages in the afternoon. She writes simple answers. People understand."

Sreejith added, "We did not spend on new machines. We spent on clearer work."

I asked Anitha if she still wanted someone to run the digital part entirely.

"No," she said. "I want someone to coach us for the next step when we are ready. Set targets, review them with us, and then step back again."

Mini framework: How to choose and work with a consultant

1. Ownership first: every account, number, and password must be in your name.

2. Teach three people: if a method cannot be taught to others beyond the owner, it is too heavy or unsustainable.

3. Floor time rule: at least half the consultant's hours should be spent on your floor, not in a meeting room.

4. Plain deliverables: write the outcome in one line, for example, batch traceability from receipt to dispatch for all pepper lots.

5. Exit plan on day one: document how you will run the process without them.

6. Staged fees: pay against working milestones, not slides, such as the first batch shipped with full traceability, the first audit passed, or the first month closed without consultant help.

7. Access log: You can see who accessed your accounts and when.

8. References you can call: speak with two clients of similar size, not just big names.

Reflection

Anitha's first question came from fatigue. She wanted someone to carry a load that felt heavier each month. The wrong consultant promised comfort but ended up building a cage. The right kind of help had the opposite effect. It stood with her on the floor, drew a clear line through the work, and then handed the chalk to her team. The work did not become modern in a grand way. It became precise, repeatable, and calm.

Consultants should be able to diagnose the issue and treat it with the proper set of tools and processes. However, before onboarding a consultant and sharing any detailed business information, conduct a reference check to ensure the consultant has relevant experience and skills in the domain and is qualified to solve your problems. A good consultant will empower you and your team to run the business independently.

Chapter 30: Wrong Guide, Billed Hourly and Daily

"Trust is built with consistency."

- **Lincoln Chafee**

The morning air in Tiruppur carried a strange mix of smells. There was the sharp edge of boiled dye from the processing units, the starch from freshly pressed shirts, and the faint aroma of filter coffee drifting from roadside stalls. Trucks had already lined up at the gates of factories. Men heaved heavy bundles of fabric onto their shoulders with practised ease. The entire industrial town moved like a living machine, every lane humming with the rhythm of sewing needles, the hiss of steam presses, and the chatter of buyers bargaining in Tamil, Hindi, and a mix of broken English.

I turned into a narrow lane that led to Vignesh Garments, a medium-sized company. The company's name was painted in bright blue letters on the outer wall, already faded under years of sun and rain.

Inside, the factory floor stretched wide with row after row of workers bent over their stations. Collars were stitched, buttons were fixed, and fabric was cut into neat stacks. Every corner carried its own beat. Supervisors walked with clipboards, shouting occasional instructions. In one corner, a tailor had placed his mobile phone near the pedal, letting music from an old film song accompany the steady whir of his machine.

Upstairs, the office looked down at the hall through a large glass panel. From there, the entire production line resembled a miniature city in motion. Behind a desk stacked with ledgers and fabric swatches sat Ms. Lakshmi Narayanan, the owner. She was in her late thirties, dressed in a crisp cotton saree, her hair neatly tied back. Her eyes, however, carried the heaviness of managing everything herself.

She greeted me politely and then wasted no time in getting to the point.

"I will be honest with you," she said, adjusting her spectacles. "I do not trust anyone who calls themselves a consultant. We had one bad experience, and since then, I refuse even to listen."

Her production manager, Aravind, a wiry man with streaks of grey in his hair, chuckled dryly. "Madam, should I tell him about the miracle men?"

She gave a slight nod, and Aravind leaned forward.

"They came with laptops and polished shoes," he began. "They spoke fast English, showed us videos of factories in Europe with glowing dashboards. They promised that in three months, our whole production and dispatch would be digital. We were impressed, and we signed the contract. Within weeks, the problems started. The workers did not understand the screens. The supervisors panicked. The so-called trainers disappeared after their second visit. Within six months, the whole system collapsed. We had to return to the ledgers. But the worst damage was not to the system; it was to our trust. We lost face."

Lakshmi added quietly, "It was not just a business failure. It killed our enthusiasm for trying anything new and embracing a more digital approach, at least through a consultant. My father had handed the reins to me. He trusted me to bring progress. Instead, the staff were confused, thinking why fix something if it wasn't broken? Customers questioned our reliability and my work style and decision capabilities. You see why I am finished with consultants and agencies?"

Her voice was steady, but her fingers tapped nervously on the table.

I let the silence stretch for a moment and then asked gently, "If one doctor gives you the wrong medicine, do you stop seeing doctors altogether?"

Lakshmi frowned. "That is different. Health is life."

Aravind, still half amused, muttered, "Business is our life too."

Lakshmi shot him a look, but I could see she was thinking.

The wound beneath the anger

I leaned forward. "Tell me honestly. What hurt more? The money lost or the feeling of being abandoned?"

Lakshmi's eyes dropped for the first time. "It was the abandonment. Money comes and goes. But when people questioned my work style and decision-making capabilities, workers were confused; when my father stayed silent during dinner, when buyers hinted that we were unreliable, that shame cut deeper than any cheque. That is why whenever someone says consultant, my blood runs cold."

Aravind nodded, his voice softer now. "After that, even the word software became a joke in this building."

Reframing the problem

I chose my words carefully. "Maybe the problem is not consultants themselves but how we choose them. What if you think of them not as miracle workers but as teachers or doctors?"

Lakshmi tilted her head, curious. "Teachers or Doctors?"

"Yes. A good teacher does not just hand you a book and leave. She makes sure you understand. She sits beside you, guiding you until you can solve the sums on your own. A bad teacher, on the other hand, gives notes and walks out. Both are called teachers, but only one earns respect. Similarly, doctors first listen, conduct check-ups, review the reports, examine the history, diagnose the problem, and then prescribe the appropriate medicine or treatment. Not directly medicine or treatment, because that worked with someone in Europe, or somewhere". I said that with a smile, and both laughed at the way it got connected with their consultant story. Thank God, with that laugh, the moment felt lighter, and I could proceed with the discussion.

Aravind said. "That is true. My maths teacher was strict, but without him I would never know how to calculate wastage rates today."

Lakshmi said. "So what you mean is that we should not reject all consultants but learn how to test them, just as we test teachers and doctors for our children and family."

"Exactly," I said.

The strange test

Aravind asked the question every businessman carries. "But how do we test them? They all look the same. Suits, laptops, presentations. You cannot tell from the first meeting."

I shared an example from a nearby hosiery unit. The owner had grown tired of empty promises, so he used a peculiar test. He asked each consultant to do one thing. Show me, in my language, how you will train my lowest-level supervisor.

Half the consultants failed on the spot. They spoke only jargon, their faces blank when asked to explain in Tamil. One consultant, however, returned the next day, gathered the foreman and two helpers, and demonstrated the process using simple cricket analogies. He said, "Think of order tracking like the scoreboard. Each entry is like a run added. If we miss one, the whole scorecard is wrong." The workers understood immediately. That consultant was hired. The system worked not because of flashy features, but because the training was relatable. Definitely, there were other selection parameters as well that they considered, which I will share with you.

Lakshmi listened intently. "So the real test is not in the slide deck. It is whether they can speak to Hari downstairs, in simple, relatable language, and make him nod with understanding."

Aravind slapped the table lightly. "Exactly. If Hari understands, everyone will follow. If he does not, we are doomed."

The first step back

Two weeks later, Lakshmi called me again. Her tone was lighter this time. "We met a new consultant. I asked him to explain his system to one of our supervisors. He did not rush. He took a fabric bundle, walked through the entry process, and even admitted when he made a mistake, correcting it. My supervisor listened carefully and then said, 'I think I can do this.' That was the first time I saw curiosity instead of fear."

Aravind joined the call, his voice firm. "And the man promised he will stay with us for six months, not just for installation. His fees are

193

tied to milestones. If we do not see results, he does not get full payment. That gave me more confidence than any software demo."

Lakshmi sighed, half-cautious and half-hopeful. "I am not ready to say I trust again. But perhaps I am ready to test."

Mini Framework: Signs of a Trustworthy Consultant or Trainer

1. They observe first. A reliable consultant spends time on your floor before suggesting solutions.

2. They train in your language. If your supervisors cannot follow, the system will collapse.

3. They link payment to results. Shared risk creates shared commitment. If it's a discussion, workshop, guidance, or strategy, an hourly, daily, or monthly rate is fine. However, you need to be clear about what you want from them.

4. They stay after installation or implementation for initial handholding. True guidance includes handholding during the messy middle.

5. Start small. A pilot project builds confidence without risking everything at once.

Reflection

Lakshmi's story is not about technology. It is about broken trust, billed at hourly, daily and monthly rates. She had every reason to be angry. Betrayal by outsiders leaves scars that do not fade easily. But she also realised that not all guides are the same. Some sell illusions, others patiently build capacity. The difference lies not in the tools they carry but, in their willingness, to understand, to teach, and to stand beside you when things get tough.

Trust, once shattered, cannot be rebuilt overnight. It returns slowly through small proofs and consistent presence. At Vignesh Garments, the sound of sewing machines remains unchanged. But the mood upstairs has shifted. The word consultant no longer means betrayal. It now means a cautious possibility, and is likened to that of a teacher or a doctor. Carefully chosen, firmly tested, and once again alive with hope.

Chapter 31: Copied Digitalisation Never Fit Well

"Don't climb the digital ladder by skipping steps. The view is best when you earn every rung."

Inspired by the real journeys of Indian MSMEs

It was mid-morning when I reached a dusty industrial lane in Rajkot, Gujarat. A slightly rusted sign outside read 'Jagruti Plastics, Household Goods.' The structure itself was more functional than formal. No glass door, no reception counter, just a corrugated iron shed that rattled each time a truck passed. Inside were two tired but loyal injection moulding machines that had seen at least ten monsoons. A thin cloud of plastic dust floated through the air like part of the furniture.

To the side, under a blue tarpaulin sheet, stood a tea stall. The chaiwala poured hot tea into small glasses without being asked. "Ram bhaiya knows who needs tea before they even arrive," joked a young worker leaning against a drum of plastic granules.

This wasn't just a workplace—it was a rhythm—a human, unspoken system.

I was here to meet Ketanbhai, the owner of the unit. A wiry man in his early forties with quick eyes and a Bluetooth earpiece that seemed permanently fixed to his left ear.

"I know I should do something digital," he said, not even waiting for introductions. "But I've already made a mistake once. I purchased this sophisticated CRM tool, which a large company was already using. Their owner had a ₹5 crore turnover, a team of engineers, and three salesmen. Me? I had one notebook and one staff member who quit the next month."

He let out a laugh, but it wasn't a joyful one.

"I didn't understand the system. My team made jokes about it. They said, 'Bhai, are we going to wear suits to work now too?' I lost ₹2,00,000, including the consultant fee. But more than that, I lost confidence. Since then, I don't want to look foolish again."

Not Copying, Just Customising

I nodded, letting his frustration settle.

"You know what the real problem was?" I asked.

He looked up, waiting.

"You tried to jump ten steps in one move. You looked at a ₹5 crore company and tried to behave like them. But you're at ₹40 lakh turnover. That's a mismatch not just of money, but of team, time, and energy."

He stayed quiet.

"If you're at ₹40 lakh," I continued, "your next inspiration should be someone at ₹60–80 lakh. What tools are *they* using? What systems have *they* cracked? Once you reach ₹60 lakh, you start looking at the ₹1 crore setups. Step by step. No skipping stairs."

He nodded slowly. "So you're saying I was solving problems I didn't even have?"

"Exactly. That CRM was meant for a team-led structure. You're still owner-driven. You need tools that respect *that* reality." Choose a better and suitable one.

The First Free Step: Internal Use First

"So what should I do now?" he asked.

"Let's start with your biggest headache. What's the one thing that eats your time every day?"

"Delivery updates," he replied instantly. "Every customer wants to know where the tempo is. I get four to five calls daily just asking the same thing."

"And what do you do?"

"I call the driver, ask him, then call the customer back. Sometimes he's out of network, and other times he forgets to update me. And I end up looking out of control."

"Okay," I said. "Let's not add more work. Let's use what you already have. Ask your tempo driver to use WhatsApp's live location feature. It's one tap. He sends it once when he starts, and it stays active for the next two hours. Customers can track where he is, and you don't have to mediate."

"That's it?"

"That's it. No new app, no form, no typing. Just a tool you already have, used smartly."

He leaned back and smiled. "That's manageable. That's real."

Climbing the Ladder—The Right Way

I could see his mindset beginning to shift. So I continued.

"You know, every business has a digital ladder. A ₹40 lakh business shouldn't implement systems like a ₹5 crore company. They don't have the same legs. But that doesn't mean they stay at the bottom."

"At ₹40 lakh, look up to ₹60–80 lakh. What are they doing digitally? Are they using WhatsApp for orders? Are they keeping records in Google Sheets? Are they sending invoices via PDF instead of paper? What CRM tools are they using?"

"Once you reach ₹60 lakh, then aim to learn from the ₹1 crore companies. Maybe then you add more digital tools with advanced CRMs or accounting and billing software."

"Then comes ₹3 crore. Then ₹10 crore. An advanced CRM will be effective when the system grows beyond your needs. But only when your team, structure, and process are ready."

He took a deep breath.

"This makes sense. No one told me this. I just thought—bigger means better."

"Bigger means different," I corrected. "Better means what's right for you right now."

Your Version, Not Their Version

I told him about a snacks seller in Madurai who uses voice typing in Tamil to track who owes how much. About a tailor in Warangal who gets more orders through WhatsApp Status than his richer competitor with a fancy website. About a honey seller in Dharamshala whose niece manages their orders through a small Telegram channel. No app. No agency. Just creativity.

He listened closely, not blinking.

"They're not copying Delhi or Mumbai," I said. "They're growing in their rhythm."

He replied, "So it's not about digital. It's about what's doable."

"Exactly."

Mini Framework: Free & Flexible Ways to Start Going Digital

Focus Area	Free Tool to Try	Why It Helps
Stock tracking	Google Sheets or any free app	Quick access, shareable, no training needed
Dispatch updates	WhatsApp Live Location or GPS location	Real-time visibility without manual effort
Orders & records	Voice-to-text applications like Google	No typing skills needed, local language friendly
Promotion	Social Media Channels, WhatsApp, Facebook, Instagram, YouTube, etc	Free visibility among existing and potential customers.
Payment	UPI, Payment Gateway, SMS or Device-based Voice confirmation	Builds trust without printed invoices

Reflection

Digital transformation is not a race. It's a relay, where you pass the baton from one milestone to the next, without skipping steps.

Ketanbhai didn't need a CRM. He needed clarity. Once he saw that growth wasn't about jumping ahead but climbing steadily, he felt lighter. More in control. More prepared.

Digital success isn't about catching up to someone else. It's about understanding where you are and growing from there.

Chapter 32: Too Many Pieces, Not Enough Pictures

"Great things are not done by impulse, but by a series of small things brought together."

- Vincent van Gogh

"Sir, which one should I follow?"

Rajeev looked up from his desk, a confused expression on his face. Arvind, his floor manager, held two sheets of paper. On one sheet, the stock of dyed yarn was listed as 412 kilos. On the other hand, it showed 385. The Excel file on Rajeev's laptop showed 397. A message from the dyeing contractor, sent last night, said 400

Rajeev pressed his fingers to his temple. "How can the same yarn weigh four different amounts?"

The office of Shree Textiles, outside Erode, felt smaller than it was. Power looms chattered in the hall beyond the glass, helpers shouted over the noise as they pushed trolleys of fabric, and a truck horn echoed from the loading bay. Inside, registers leaned against a stack of files. A laptop blinked with too many tabs open. Two phones vibrated on the table, one with customer messages, the other with supplier updates.

"This is my reality," Rajeev said, turning to me. "People keep telling me to integrate. But look at what I already have. Bits of digital are everywhere, and none of them agree. If I try to consolidate everything into one system, it will collapse. At least this mess is a mess I know."

Arvind cleared his throat. "Sir, the contractor called. He asked why we want another delivery when the last lot is already in the godown. I did not know what to say."

Rajeev shut his eyes for a second. "This is exactly how we lose face."

The weight of fragments

I asked Rajeev to walk me through a typical day. He woke at six and scanned messages in three supplier groups. He checked one stock file on his laptop and another kept by the supervisor. He met his accountant at six in the evening to match numbers again. Three places for the same truth, and none of them matched.

"My father ran this place with two registers," he said, tapping the old ledger near his elbow. "The moment we opened the door to half digital, half paper, we got stuck in between. If this is digital, I want no part of it."

Kavita, his wife, stepped in with a cup of tea. "Last year, I told him to buy a big system that a cousin recommended. When he saw the price, he put the brochure away. And even if we paid, we would still need people who can sit in front of screens all day. Our boys are good at fabric and deadlines, not dropdown menus."

Rajeev nodded. "I would rather be called old-fashioned than buy something that fails and makes me look like a fool."

Breaking the wall into bricks

"What gives you the most pain every day," I asked, "not in theory, but in your stomach?"

He did not answer quickly. Outside, a worker called for the gate to be opened, and metal scraped on concrete.

"Dispatch confusion," he said at last. "Yarn stock that goes missing on paper. Payments that keep slipping and turn into awkward calls. If I fix just those three, I can breathe."

"Then that is the order," I said. "Not everything. Not an overhaul. One knot at a time. Think of a wall that looks crooked. You do not rebuild the house. You take out the worst bricks and set them right."

Kavita leaned forward. "Where do we start first?"

"Where it hurts most," I said. "Dispatch and stock must agree. Forget everything else for now."

First step: one sheet everyone can see

That afternoon, Rajeev called Arvind and two supervisors into the office. Together, we made a single sheet on the office computer with four clear fields: order number, customer name, dispatch date, and status. No extra columns. No formulas that needed an expert. One person filled it out throughout the day, and Sunita from accounts read it at 5:00 p.m. and ticked off what was complete.

The first week was full of mistakes. An order was entered twice. Another was missed entirely. Rajeev frowned and said it would be easier to return to the diary. Sunita shook her head. "At least now I can see the mistake before the truck leaves. Earlier, I saw it a week later."

By the third week, the mistakes had reduced. The team began to look at the same screen instead of shuffling papers. Arguments became conversations. A pattern began to emerge from the noise.

Second step: yarn without guesswork

Next, we touched yarn. Three ledgers had three numbers for the same shade. Rajeev's son, who visited on weekends from Coimbatore, built a simple file with three colours. Green meant enough stock. Yellow meant reorder soon. Red meant urgent. The production manager updated it every Friday before leaving for the weekend.

On the first Friday, he grumbled that he had no time for this. On the third Friday, he said, without being asked, "We will need more of the navy shade by Wednesday." Rajeev smiled at me later. "I did not have to call five suppliers in a panic. I called two and got a better rate."

Third step: money that does not hide

For payments, Sunita decided not to digitise the whole history. She entered only the invoices that had crossed their due date. Rajeev now had a small, clear list of names to call each Tuesday afternoon. The list was short enough to act on. It stopped being a sea of files and became a manageable handful of numbers that he could complete in an hour.

"Earlier I felt blind," Sunita said.

The stress test arrives.

The real test came without warning. A buyer from Surat placed a rush order for sweaters in three sizes and two colours, with a delivery deadline that would usually make Rajeev say no. Ten minutes later, a Delhi distributor asked to prepone his dispatch by four days. At the same time, the dyeing contractor called to say that one shade would be late by twenty-four hours due to a fault in his heating line.

In the old days, this was the moment when Rajeev would pull a chair onto the floor and not leave it for the next two nights. He would stand over every table, signing slips, checking cartons, and yelling above the looms until his voice went hoarse.

This time, he stayed in the doorway of the office and watched.

Arvind opened the dispatch sheet and read out what was due the next day. The supervisor on the floor repeated it back to him. The yarn file showed where they stood. The navy shade was yellow, not red, so they had room to reshuffle without breaking the line. A junior moved two small orders out by a day with quick calls and noted the change on the same sheet. Sunita checked the overdue list and called a buyer who owed them money. The payment arrived by evening. That cash cleared a supplier's bill and ensured the workers' wages were paid on time.

There were mistakes. A carton meant for Delhi picked up a label for Erode city. Arvind caught it when he scanned the list and corrected it at the table. A helper incorrectly labelled the size on a bundle tag. The supervisor checked against the dispatch sheet and sent the bundle back for a fresh tag before loading it onto the truck.

At eight thirty, the truck rolled out. Rajeev watched the back doors close and waited for his chest to unclench. He realised it already had.

"I did not sleep in the office," he said quietly. "I did not even raise my voice. The workers knew what to do."

What the team learned

The next morning, we stood by the glass, gazing at the floor. Rajeev pointed at the old ledger. "We did not throw it away. It still holds signatures that matter. But the daily fight is not in there anymore."

206

Arvind spoke up. "We did not become software experts. We just stopped hiding the truth in five places."

Sunita added, "I like that I can step in and help without running to the godown. If Rajeev is out, the work still moves."

Kavita smiled. "Last night he came home before dinner."

Rajeev laughed and shook his head. "First time in the Diwali season."

Mini framework: a staggered path out of fragments

1. Pick three pains you feel every week. Do not guess. Dispatch, stock, and overdue payments are common.

2. Resolve one pain point with a single shared source of truth. A single sheet is enough to begin.

3. Put names to tasks. One fills, one reviews. Everyone can read.

4. Hold the line for three months. Do not add new tools while the habit forms.

5. Add the next layer only when the first runs without drama.

6. Train two employees for every digital step to ensure continuity when one person is away.

7. Measure one visible win per layer, such as fewer last-minute shortages or one less night spent at the factory.

Reflection

Rajeev feared integration because he imagined a leap into a system he could neither afford nor control. What worked was not a leap but a sequence. A single place for dispatch truth. A simple colour signal for yarn. A short list of money that must come in. The tools were ordinary. The order was 'the change.' Once there was order, the business began to feel larger on the inside than it looked on the outside. He was already using digital tools, but they were not integrated, and together, it was chaos. Digital in isolation or silos often results in chaos if not integrated well. It's not just about using digital tools, but using them in a way that integrates different sources to present the correct picture and aid in making the best decision.

Chapter 33: Closing the Digital Loop of the Chain

"If you want to change the world, start with yourself."

- *Mahatma Gandhi*

By the time I reached Indore's grain mandi, the yard was already heaving with activity. Trucks were parked in a crooked line, engines idling while labourers dragged heavy sacks across the ground. Auctions echoed from one corner, and the air was thick with the earthy smell of wheat and chana.

Ravi Gupta's wholesale grain shop was wedged between two others, its walls lined with gunny bags stacked so high they seemed to touch the ceiling. A small wooden counter sat at the front, crowded with registers, a calculator, and a chipped glass of tea going cold.

Ravi greeted me with a weary smile. His shirt sleeves were rolled up, and a fine dust of grain clung to his hair. "I will tell you my problem directly," he said. "I am ready to go digital. My son has been pushing me. But unless my suppliers and customers are also ready, what is the point? I cannot be digital alone. The loop will stay open."

As if on cue, his son Sameer came in, carrying two hot cups of tea. He was in his twenties, sharp-eyed, and clearly eager. "Papa is right," he said. "I tried setting up an app for invoicing. But when the dal mill sends us only hand-written slips, I have to enter them manually. And when we send digital invoices to some shopkeepers, they ignore them and continue to request paper bills. We end up doing double work. Where is the benefit?"

Ravi shook his head. "This is what I mean. If I change and they don't, I will appear foolish for doing extra work. I already tried once. People still remind me of it."

The Sting of the Past

I asked him what he meant. Ravi sighed. "Five years ago, I bought an accounting and billing software. The consultant trained my nephew, but none of my suppliers agreed to send bills digitally. And my customers, especially the older ones, refused to look at emailed invoices. After a year, I dropped it. My staff laughed and said I wasted money trying to act modern. Even today, I feel the sting."

Sameer added, "That is why I am hesitant. I do not want Papato to face the same humiliation again."

This was not a reluctance to adopt digital. It was the scar of failure, the memory of being mocked for trying to modernise when the value chain is not digital and ready.

Breaking the Myth

I leaned closer and asked, "Do you really believe every supplier and every customer must be convinced before you begin?"

Ravi replied firmly, "Of course. Otherwise, how will the chain close?"

"That is a myth," I said gently. "Digital adoption is not a rope where everyone must pull together at the same time. It is a wheel. If you start turning the wheel in your shop, others will eventually have to catch up because it will make their life easier."

Ravi looked doubtful. Sameer frowned. "But we will still be stuck doing both, digital and manual."

"Yes, for a short time," I agreed. "But if you begin with yourself and make the benefit visible, suppliers and customers will slowly ask for it themselves. Not because you forced them, but because they saw the advantage."

A Simple Experiment

We decided to try an experiment. Sameer picked three younger customers in Ujjain who were already using WhatsApp and Digital payments. Instead of giving them only paper slips, he sent both a digital invoice on WhatsApp and a hard copy.

On the supplier side, Ravi tried another approach. With one supplier, he said politely, "If you can email me the invoice, I will process your payment faster." The supplier hesitated but agreed to give it a try. With the others, Ravi scanned their paper bills into his own system, keeping digital records consistent.

After a week, Sameer showed his father a small report. "For the first time, I can see daily sales totals in one click," he said. Ravi looked at the printout with surprise. "This is what I wanted a few years ago. But still, the loop is not closed."

The First Signs of Change

Two weeks later, I returned to the shop. Sameer looked excited. "One of the Ujjain shopkeepers called me," he said. "He told me the digital invoice helped him compare prices easily. He said, Send it every time. It actually made him prefer us."

Ravi raised his eyebrows. "So now the customer is asking for it?"

"Yes," Sameer nodded. "And I told him we can also send monthly statements digitally. He was very happy. Do you see, Papa? They are starting to step into our circle."

On the supplier side, something else had shifted. A dal mill that earlier refused to change now sends PDFs regularly because Ravi linked it with faster payments. "They realised it is in their interest," Ravi admitted.

The Turning Point

The real test came when a bulk buyer from Bhopal placed an urgent order for soy. Usually, this would have caused chaos with calculators and registers flying. But this time, Sameer processed the order entirely digitally, generated the invoice, and shared a digital copy of the challan with a date and timestamp.

When the buyer called to ask about delivery, Sameer replied calmly, "Please check the document I shared on WhatsApp and email. All details are there."

The buyer responded, "Your system is cleaner than others. Next month, I will increase my order."

That evening, Ravi looked at me with a different expression. "Now I understand. Digital does not begin by convincing others and waiting for others to change. It begins with me. If I show the value, they will join because it benefits them."

Mini Framework: Closing the Open Loop

Step	Action	Why It Works
1	Begin with yourself and staff	Builds internal confidence and consistency
2	Select a few ready customers	Early wins show visible benefits
3	Incentivise suppliers	Faster payments create cooperation
4	Keep both systems briefly	Reduces resistance during transition
5	Share success stories	Others follow when they see proof

Reflection

Ravi once believed that digital adoption was impossible unless every supplier and every customer moved in tandem. What he discovered was the opposite. By beginning in his own shop, he created a ripple. Customers liked the convenience. Suppliers preferred faster payments for the sake of process speed and clarity. His staff liked fewer midnight calculations.

Change management is not about dragging everyone forward; it's about guiding them. It is about leading quietly from the centre until others realise it is in their interest to join. That is how you take charge of your business and legacy.

Chapter 34: Passing the Baton

"None of us is as smart as all of us."

- **Ken Blanchard**

The lane outside Howrah's wholesale spice market wakes up in layers. First, the porters come with burlap sacks wobbling from their shoulders. Then the tea boys weave through the crowd, suspending aluminium kettles on trays, steam curling into the morning air. Finally, shutters roll up one by one, and the market hum begins.

The smell is impossible to mistake, turmeric dust seized in the sunlight, roasted jeera wafting from a nearby mill, and somewhere a whiff of cardamom. Shukla Masala Stores sits halfway down the lane, a narrow shop with shelves like tall bookcases, each cubby filled with the colours of a kitchen.

Suresh Shukla was waiting at the entrance. Tall, careful in his movements, he spoke with the same precision he used when mixing spice blends. His wife, Meera, sat on a stool near the doorway, a cloth purse at her side and a small calculator in her hand. The foreman, Hari, was tying shipment tags to gunny bags stacked against the wall. Two packers, Manoj and Alok, were folding brown paper cones for retail orders. In one corner, the nephew, a young man in a checked shirt, leaned over his phone as a Bluetooth printer spat out labels.

Once we settled behind the desk, worn smooth by decades of ledgers, Suresh said, without ceremony, "When people talk about technology, I tell them my nephew handles it. He is faster. I am not. But when he is not here, we are stuck."

Meera didn't look up from her cash tally. "Last month, the payment app froze," she said. "Customers were waiting. The nephew had gone to his village. We called him again and again. When he answered, he told me, 'Maami, press this, then this.' It still didn't work. I felt foolish in front of customers who trust us."

From the doorway, Hari added, "The lorry was ready, but we couldn't generate the invoice. We wrote the details on paper and sent the goods. The whole time, I worried something would go wrong."

Suresh rubbed the edge of the desk with his thumb, his voice quieter now. "That day, I realised our problem is not technology. Our problem is dependency."

A Different Way to Look at the Team

I didn't start with software demos or app names; instead, I aimed to understand and document the situation on paper, allowing me to see the challenge. I pulled out a plain sheet of paper and drew three columns: Who is curious? What do they already do? What small tool can they own?

Suresh read the headings and nodded. Curiosity we have. We just need a path."

We looked around the room.

Meera had already balanced cash and tallied credit notes. She agreed to learn the basic billing screen and save daily backups to the family email. She laughed and said, "If I could balance the gift list at my sister's wedding, I can manage two buttons here."

Hari knew every driver by first name and remembered which route had a bridge under repair. He agreed to handle delivery updates. Instead of making ten phone calls, he would share his live location in a small WhatsApp group with the customer and the store. During the trial run, the phone buzzed on the counter, and the tiny blue dot on the map made everyone lean in and laugh.

Manoj, fresh out of school and quick with his phone, offered to scan supplier bills and file them in month-wise folders on Google Drive. He tested it by scanning an old invoice and naming it correctly.

Alok, older and quieter, kept a small diary noting which blends sold best on which days. We asked him to try Google Voice Artificial Intelligence (AI) Typing in Hindi so his notes could be shared instantly. He spoke into the mic, watched the words appear, and grinned. "If it understands my accent, it can understand anyone."

I said, do you want to learn that with consent, this application could also analyse which days' sales were how much, estimate the sales for the next few weeks based on past data and also tell which customer has been ordering what, how much and in which week or month. You can plan better and reach out to your customers in advance. No need to remember. This AI-based application can do wonders for your business, and we have just begun testing and exploring its capabilities.

Suresh took the last slot himself. He would learn only one thing for now: how to open the billing app, take a backup, and restore the previous day's data.

The nephew watched all this with a mix of amusement and relief. "If everyone can do a little," he said, "I can spend time improving things instead of being the emergency helpline."

Learning in the Middle of Work

We set aside fifteen minutes each afternoon, when the market was quietest. There was no training room, no projector, just the same desk, the same phones, and a straightforward task per person.

The first week was awkward. Meera forgot to attach the backup once. Hari posted his live location in the wrong group, and his relatives began tracking him while he was on a tea break. Manoj scanned a bill upside down. Alok spoke too softly, and his voice notes turned into gibberish. Suresh pressed the wrong option and shut down the app entirely.

Each mistake became a small story, and each story made the next attempt easier.

By the second week, these small jobs felt like part of the shop's rhythm. On a busy Friday, the nephew left early. A customer wanted a duplicate invoice from last month. Meera opened the drive folder and found it in seconds. Hari sent an update to a nervous new client. Manoj fetched a supplier bill for the accountant without searching through piles of paper. Alok's sales notes showed that Fridays needed more counter staff. Suresh ran the backup before closing and went home without worry.

A Test During Festival Rush

The real test came during Diwali week. The market was a blur of colour and noise: gold-foil packaging spilling from cartons, customers crowding at the counter, delivery boys weaving through the lane with stacks of boxes.

By mid-morning, the nephew had to leave for a supply issue at the warehouse. An urgent bulk order arrived from a sweet shop that needed extra masala blends before the evening. The customer was in a rush and wanted a printed invoice before paying.

A month ago, this would have caused panic.

Meera handled billing, tapping in the items and printing the invoice without hesitation. Hari updated the customer in the WhatsApp group with an estimated delivery time and live location once the goods left. Manoj scanned the supplier bill for that batch and stored it before sealing the cartons. Alok reviewed his notes and suggested adding a second blend that the customer frequently purchased during Diwali. Suresh ran the backup at the end, making sure every record was secure before the next rush.

The order was dispatched in thirty minutes. The customer sent a voice note: "Your service is as good as your spices." Everyone laughed, but they all knew the relay team had worked.

Why Three-Five Champions Matter for a Micro business

One person who knows everything is helpful until they are absent. Three to five people who each know something create a safety net. Customers stay informed. The owner stays calm. Technology becomes a shared tool, not a guarded secret.

I have seen this work across India: a mother and son in Coimbatore who alternate sending end-of-day WhatsApp summaries; a leather unit in Kanpur where the cutter uploads weekly stock photos; a bakery in Shillong where four staff handle digital payments, ending queues at rush hour. Different trades, same lesson, do not build one hero, create a relay team.

Mini Framework: Building Your Five Tech Champions

Step	What to Do	How to Keep It Simple
1	Pick the curious three to five employees	Choose people who ask questions during the day
2	Give one tool per person	Billing backup, live location, scanning, inventory tools, voice notes, and drive folders
3	Train in the flow of work	Ten to fifteen minutes at the quietest time
4	Write it where everyone can see	A paper chart on the wall shows who does what, and others also try to teach and learn other tools.
5	Rotate one task every quarter	Prevents dependence and keeps skills fresh
6	Celebrate small saves	Thank people when their action avoided a problem

Reflection

Suresh once thought technology decisions belonged to the person who understood it best. He still respects that skill, but now he knows the real strength lies in spreading it. The shop has not lost its soul;

instead, it has changed its habits. Five people now carry part of the system, and that feels like air flowing through a once-closed room.

On my last visit before Durga Puja, Meera handed me a packet of freshly ground garam masala and said, "Now when the phone rings, I do not panic." Hari grinned and showed me the day's delivery group on his phone. The nephew leaned in the doorway, looking lighter. Suresh rolled down the shutter and said quietly, "Tomorrow can come."

Section 5: Incentives & Growth Pathways

Why should MSMEs embrace digital, beyond survival? Because it opens doors to growth opportunities that are otherwise out of reach. From government schemes to IPO dreams, from preserving legacy to scaling like industry peers, digital becomes the bridge between "small today" and "big tomorrow." This section inspires MSMEs with examples and incentives, shifting the narrative from cost to investment.

Chapter 35: A Door That Opens Wider

"Growth is never by mere chance. It is the result of forces working together."

- *N. R. Narayana Murthy*

Bhagalpur in Bihar is famous for its tussar silk. Walk through the lanes and you hear the sound of looms clacking inside homes. Long threads stretch across courtyards, children play between bundles of yarn, and older weavers sit with nimble fingers tying knots. In one such house, I met Abdul Rahman, a man in his fifties who had spent his life weaving saris. His loom stood in the centre of the room, occupying as much space as a bed.

Rahman's face showed both pride and fatigue. He loved his work but was tired of the struggle. "Everyone tells me to go digital," he said, adjusting the thread on his loom. "They say put your saris online, use e-commerce. I ask them, how? I do not have a computer. I do not know English. If I go to the government for help, it will be years of waiting. Files move slowly, officials ask for signatures, and then more papers are required. I tried once before and got nothing. Why should I try again?"

His wife, seated nearby with spools of thread, added, "Last time he went to the office ten times. Each visit meant lost work. In the end, the file disappeared. Nothing came."

The frustration in their voices was not just about money. It was about dignity. For Rahman, government schemes had always felt like distant promises locked away in offices.

Memories of Disappointment

Rahman recalled his earlier attempt. "I applied for a loan under the handloom scheme. I filled every form, stood in long queues, and carried documents in a plastic folder. I visited the office multiple times. After four months, the officer told me it would take more time. That day I decided, never again. Better to struggle on my own than run around in corridors."

His neighbour, a younger weaver named Imran, joined our conversation. Imran had a different story. "Rahman bhai, I know you lost hope. But last year, my cousin got support for a solar loom. He applied online through the Common Service Centre in our village. Yes, it took three months, but he got the subsidy. His electricity bill has halved."

Rahman shook his head. "Maybe your cousin was lucky. For most of us, schemes are talk."

His words echoed the mistrust of thousands of micro entrepreneurs across India.

A Small Workshop in Surat

Weeks later, I met Seema Patel in Surat, Gujarat. She ran a small garment stitching unit with twenty women working under her. Rolls of cloth were stacked along the walls, and the sound of sewing machines filled the workshop.

Seema too had doubts about schemes. "They say the government gives support for digital machines and ERP systems," she said. "But who has the time to chase and check websites? Consultants charge money. I have to run this workshop every day. If I spend weeks on paperwork, who will manage production?"

Her hesitation was not anger, but exhaustion. Yet, despite her doubts, she had applied for a scheme that reimbursed part of the cost of digital tools.

"To my surprise," she admitted, "it was not as difficult as I thought. Everything was online. I had to upload Aadhaar, PAN, and GST details. After submission, I got a message confirming my application. Three months later, the reimbursement came directly to my account. That helped me pay for the accounting software we use now."

She smiled as she showed me the software on her computer. "I realise now the schemes are real. But we need patience and the right guidance. Without that, people give up halfway."

The Medium Enterprise Perspective

In Tiruppur, Tamil Nadu, where knitwear factories line entire streets, I met Karthik, the owner of a medium-sized export unit. His turnover was nearly one hundred and eighty crore, and his factory employed more than two hundred workers.

"When GST was introduced," he said, "we were confused. Compliance was heavy. My staff made errors, and we paid penalties. I thought that if we asked for government training, it would lead to endless bureaucracy. But then we tried a digital training scheme supported by the Ministry of MSME. Trainers came to our factory and taught our staff step by step, enabling us to file smoothly within weeks. I had expected piles of paperwork. Instead, it was handled online and was much simpler than I imagined."

Karthik leaned back in his chair, thoughtful. "The schemes are like doors. They do not open by themselves. You have to knock properly, with the right documents and patience. But once open, they give real help."

A Change of Heart

Back in Bhagalpur, Rahman's daughter persuaded him to at least try a small digital training program funded under a government scheme. She registered him at the Common Service Centre. The confirmation message arrived on his phone.

Rahman looked at it skeptically. "If this works, I will believe things have changed. But I will not waste endless visits again."

Weeks later, after attending the training, Rahman admitted something unexpected. "It was not easy for me, but the trainers spoke in Hindi, and they showed me how to take photos of my saris and upload them. I realised it is possible. I still prefer my loom to any phone, but maybe the schemes are not all empty talk."

The shift was small, but it mattered. For someone who had sworn never to try again, he had taken a step forward.

Mini Framework: Making Government Schemes Work

1. Start with the smallest scheme. Apply first for training or reimbursements, not for big loans.

2. Use local support centres. Common Service Centres and district MSME offices now help with online applications.

3. Prepare documents in advance. Aadhaar, PAN, GST, and basic bank details are sufficient to get started.

4. Ask peers who succeeded. Learn from other entrepreneurs in your industry and associations rather than relying on rumours.

5. Stay patient but persistent. Timelines can stretch, but most schemes deliver if appropriately followed.

Reflection

Across micro, small, and medium enterprises, the initial response to government schemes is one of mistrust. Old memories of lost files, endless signatures, and wasted trips discourage many from even trying. Yet the landscape is changing. Many applications are online. Support reaches directly into bank accounts. Training sessions come to the factory floor.

Schemes are not miracles. They will not transform a business overnight. But they are resources waiting to be tapped. Those who approach with the right mindset, documents ready, and patience intact often discover that the doors do open.

Rahman in Bhagalpur, Seema in Surat, and Karthik in Tiruppur all began with doubts. Each discovered in their own way that government schemes do not replace their effort. They amplify it. They reduce cost, provide training, and make the journey to digital smoother.

The lesson is simple. Government support is not about taking control of your business. It is about placing tools in your hands, tools that you must still use with your skill and discipline.

Chapter 36: The Cost of Waiting

"The cost of doing nothing is far more than the cost of change."

By many veterans

In the industrial belt of Gujarat, Ketan Industries stood as a monument to its founder's principles. Mr. Ketan Patel, a man whose life's work was etched into the grime and steel of his factory, believed in the permanence of tangible things. For forty years, his business had churned out precise automotive components using a blend of old, formidable presses and the unshakeable expertise of his workforce. The air was thick with the scent of machining oil, and every gear and piston seemed to hum a song of endurance. His business was profitable, his contracts secure, and he saw no reason to invite chaos.

I watched him inspect a newly forged part, a glint of pride in his eyes. "We have never missed a deadline," he told me, "and our quality is second to none. My son talks to me about 'digital' this and 'robotics' that. I say to him, Why? I have not received any government offers or support for digital shifts. No perks, no push. Why should I spend crores on new machines and software? My business is a success because of hard work, not some virtual reality. I will wait until they offer us a good deal, a tax break, or some kind of incentive. Why risk a profitable business for something so uncertain?"

Mr. Patel's apprehension was not born of fear, but of a deep-seated pragmatism and reliance on government incentives and subsidies. He was a businessman who saw digital transformation as a luxury, not a necessity. He believed that if the government truly wanted him to modernise, it would offer a clear, financially justifiable incentive. Until then, he was content to operate on his own terms, with his own reliable machines, and a belief that his legacy was secure. His greatest strength, his stability, was about to become his greatest vulnerability.

The Unseen Threat: A Quiet Ultimatum

The threat came not from a rival factory, but in the quiet, sterile form of a Vendor Quality Audit. The client, a global automotive giant, sent a team to assess Mr. Patel's factory. They walked the floors, meticulously recording every process. They praised his craftsmanship but raised questions about traceability and quality assurance. Mr. Patel's hand-written logs and manual inspections were a point of concern. The audit report, a few days later, was a diplomatic but devastating document.

"While we appreciate your dedication to quality," the report stated, "our new global standards require real-time data integration, end-to-end traceability, and a full digital twin of your manufacturing process." The term was a foreign language to Mr. Patel. The report concluded with a chilling line: "Failure to meet these new metrics will regrettably result in a reassessment of our partnership."

The ultimatum landed like a physical blow. Losing this client would mean a catastrophic loss of revenue and, more importantly, a loss of the reputation he had spent a lifetime building. He had been so focused on what the government wasn't giving him that he hadn't noticed what his own market was demanding. He realised with a sinking feeling that the world was not waiting for a handout; it was moving on, leaving him behind.

His son, Soham, saw this as the critical moment to act. He had been a champion of modernisation, but now he had the leverage he needed. "Dad," he said, holding the report, "the biggest incentive is right here. It's the cost of not modernising. We don't need a cash handout. We need a way to prove our quality. The problem isn't the technology; it's our mindset."

The New Outlook: Proactive, Not Passive

Soham's solution was not just to buy new machines; it was to use the very tools Mr. Patel had dismissed as toys to save the business. He had spent months researching government initiatives, and he presented a compelling case: the government wasn't just giving away money, it was providing a strategic framework for those who were willing to take the leap. The mindset shift was from waiting for incentives to proactively leveraging them.

- The Right Technology: The plan involved a comprehensive digital transformation to create an accurate Industry 4.0 model. The first step was to install IoT sensors on every machine. These sensors would collect real-time data on temperature, pressure, vibration, and output, feeding it all into a central dashboard. This stream of data would become the foundation of their new, intelligent factory.

- Building the Digital Twin: Soham explained the digital twin in terms a pragmatist could understand. "It's a virtual copy of our factory. We can test new production lines, optimise machine layouts, and find hidden inefficiencies on a computer, without ever having to shut down the factory. It's like having a crystal ball that shows us the future of our production." This virtual model would allow them to run simulations and achieve a level of precision that was impossible with human-led processes.

- Automating for Precision: To meet the client's high-volume, high-precision demands, they would integrate several robotic arms into the production line. These robots would handle repetitive, high-volume tasks with flawless accuracy, freeing up their skilled workers for more complex, creative tasks like quality control and machine maintenance.

Leveraging Government Schemes

Soham then laid out the financial roadmap, proving that the incentives Mr. Patel had been waiting for were already in place. He pointed to the SAMARTH Udyog Bharat initiative, a nationwide drive to push for advanced manufacturing. He demonstrated how the company could apply for interest subsidies on loans for technology upgrades, thereby drastically reducing its financial burden. He also discovered a state-specific scheme in Gujarat that offered tax benefits and expedited clearances for companies adopting robotics and automation. The biggest incentive, he argued, was not in a tax break, but in the access to new, higher-value markets that this transformation would unlock. The government actively promoted and connected modernised factories with large international buyers who were seeking technologically advanced suppliers.

The financial argument was irrefutable. The cost of not investing was losing their largest contract. The cost of investing was offset by the very incentives Mr. Patel had been waiting for. He realised with a sense of both dread and excitement that he had been standing still while the world moved forward, and that his traditional wisdom was no longer enough. The fear of a multi-crore investment was now replaced by the much greater fear of losing it all.

The ROI: From Stagnation to Strategic Advantage

The transformation was a monumental undertaking, but the results were almost immediate.

- Enhanced Resilience: The IoT sensors allowed them to catch a looming machine failure in a stamping press weeks in advance, preventing a costly breakdown and production halt.

- Flawless Quality: The digital twin allowed them to test new processes virtually, achieving a level of precision that surpassed their client's requirements. The robotic arms handled the most delicate tasks with perfect consistency, reducing defects to near zero.

- New Market Access: They not only retained their existing contract but also impressed the global client with their digital transformation, which led to connections with other manufacturers in their supply chain. Mr. Patel's factory, once a stable but stagnant legacy, was now a shining example of a modern Indian enterprise. They secured two new, high-margin contracts for parts they couldn't have even considered making before.

Mr. Patel, who had once seen digital transformation as a costly, unrewarded venture, now saw it as the only way to stay competitive. He learned that the government incentive was already there; he just did not explore it enough or sought help, he was living in denial. He had been so focused on what he could get from the government directly rather than building a strategic advantage for his business. Now he thinks, what if he had implemented this earlier? His company would have gone to the next level, maybe even preparing for his dream to go public through the IPO.

Mini-Framework: The Mindset Shift from Inactive to Proactive

- The Threat is Real: Understand that your market is not waiting for you to change. Your biggest competitors may be across the globe, and your biggest clients are adopting new, technology-driven standards.

- Look Beyond Direct Subsidies: Recognise that government incentives are a strategic framework, not a simple cash handout. They come in the form of interest subsidies, reimbursements, tax benefits, and access to new markets.

- Embrace Proactive Investment: Change your mindset from waiting for a "push" to actively seeking out and leveraging the resources that are already available. The government's role is not to lead; it's to support those who are ready to take the first step.

- The New Metric of ROI: The return on investment for digital transformation isn't just in cost savings. It's in resilience, strategic advantage, and the ability to compete on a global stage.

Reflection

Mr. Ketan Patel's journey is a powerful case study for a different kind of apprehension. His resistance was not to the technology itself, but to the perceived lack of a clear financial incentive. He had a traditional, prudent mindset that believed in a direct, one-to-one exchange: "I invest, you subsidise." He failed to see that the digital ecosystem was an entirely new game with different rules. The government's role had shifted from simply giving handouts to providing a framework for those who were willing to take the lead. His transformation wasn't about him changing his core belief in profitability; it was about him realising that a new, more proactive approach to business was now required to secure it.

Chapter 37: Be the First in the Lane

"The person who follows the crowd will usually go no further than the crowd. The person who walks alone is likely to find himself in places no one has ever been before."

- **Albert Einstein**

The winter sun had just started softening the chill in Moradabad's old brass market. Every lane was alive with the music of work, the hollow ring of hammer on metal, the scrape of files against brass, the thud of a chisel carving floral designs. Coal stoves hissed outside workshops where men warmed their hands between tasks. The air carried a mix of metal dust and sweet chai from the tea stalls tucked into corners.

I stopped at a narrow shop with a faded wooden board: *Ashfaq and Sons, Brass Engraving*. Inside, brass plates gleamed under the yellow light. Ashfaq sat cross-legged on a low stool, bent over a half-finished tray, tapping out a pattern with a chisel so fine it looked like lacework.

He looked up when I stepped in, set his chisel down, and gestured to a stool in the corner.

"You are here to talk about these modern business ideas?" he asked.

"Has Anyone Like Me Grown with Digital?"

233

As I sat down, Ashfaq asked the question he had ready before I arrived.

"In my trade, have you met anyone who has grown using digital? Not exporters. Not big showrooms. I mean a small shop like mine, selling to traders and customers who already know me."

I thought for a moment. "No, I haven't met someone exactly in your trade who has done it."

He gave a small, satisfied smile. "So why should I try? If no one else has done it, maybe it doesn't work for people like me."

The chaiwala from across the lane called out, asking if we wanted tea. Ashfaq ordered two cups, and while we waited, I leaned forward.

"When no one has done it, that doesn't always mean it won't work. Sometimes it means there's space for you to be the first. Others will point to you when they see it working."

Ashfaq chuckled, shaking his head. "You talk like I can be an example for the whole lane."

"You can," I replied, "if you start with something that fits into the work you already do."

The tea arrived, hot and milky. We sat in the warm steam for a moment before I asked, "How do you keep track of special designs for customers?"

"In my head," he said, tapping his temple. "If a customer comes after six months, I can still match their order."

"And if you are not here for a week?"

He hesitated. Outside, a cart wheel squeaked past, and a hammer struck metal in a steady rhythm.

"My son or my worker would guess," he admitted.

"That's where you can start," I said. "No need for websites or ads. Just take a photo of each custom order before it leaves the shop. Save it in a folder with the customer's name and date. Anyone can find it if you are not here."

A week later, I visited again. Ashfaq's phone sat on the counter, open to a gallery of brass trays and bowls. Each photo had a customer's name in the caption.

"My son showed me how to add the names," he said, flipping through the gallery. "Yesterday, a trader from Lucknow sent his cousin here. He wanted a bigger tray than the one we made last month. I found the photo in seconds and took the order."

The satisfaction in his voice was quiet but clear.

Two weeks later, I came during the run-up to Eid. The lane was packed with buyers, delivery boys carrying stacks of trays wrapped in paper, and shopkeepers calling out to each other.

Inside Ashfaq's shop, two workers polished brass while his son packed an order. A man walked in, holding a photo on his phone. His brother in Bareilly had bought a vase from Ashfaq and wanted another one exactly like it.

Ashfaq handed the phone to his son, who opened the gallery, matched the design, confirmed the size, and gave a delivery date, all in under two minutes. The customer placed the order without hesitation.

As the man left, Ashfaq glanced at me and said, "You were right. No one else here can do this so quickly."

Mini Framework: How to Start When No One Else Has

Step	Action	Why It Matters
1	Accept being the first	No competition yet in your lane
2	Pick a habit that fits your work rhythm	Easy to maintain daily
3	Record your output	Helps with repeat and referral orders
4	Make it accessible to family or staff	Work doesn't pause if you are away
5	Let results speak	Customers value efficiency without marketing

Reflection

Ashfaq's first reaction was to dismiss the idea because no one like him had done it before. But that absence turned out to be his advantage. By adopting a habit simple enough to keep up, he made his work easier for himself, his son, and his customers.

In a trade where reputation spreads through word of mouth, being the first to add a layer of speed and certainty gave him a quiet edge over his peers.

Chapter 38: From the Shop Floor to the Stock Exchange

"Coming together is a beginning; keeping together is progress; working together is success."

— Henry Ford

By the time the sun climbed over the coconut groves outside Coimbatore, the industrial lane in Ganapathy was already wide awake. Tea sellers balanced steel tumblers as they hurried between workshops, the hiss of idlis steaming in the corner shop mixed with the steady rumble of lathes starting up for the day.

Anitha Gears & Components stood at the centre of it all, a cream-painted factory with blue shutters and its name hand-painted in bold letters. From the road, it looked like a dozen other units, but inside was a carefully tuned orchestra. Sparks from welding flashed in one corner, the smell of cutting oil hung in the air, and workers in blue overalls moved in a rhythm they had practised for years.

From her glass-walled cabin overlooking the floor, Anitha Rajendran could see every station. On her desk were neat towers of files, a cold tumbler of filter coffee, and a wall calendar covered with pencilled delivery dates.

When I sat down across from her, she didn't waste time.

"We've grown from four machines to forty in fifteen years," she said, her voice steady but with the weight of long days in it. "Now my CA says that if we want to go public in three years, we need to 'digitally prepare' the business. I understand machines. I understand people. But stock exchanges? That feels like another world."

Her operations manager, Murugan, entered with the day's production report, thick green paper, the kind that smells faintly of ink and dust. Anitha flipped through it without really looking, like someone scanning a familiar recipe.

"This," she said, holding it up, "is how I have always worked. But they tell me investors will want live dashboards, standardised formats, and traceable records."

She hesitated before adding, "Part of me worries... what if going digital exposes every inefficiency we've just lived with all these years? What if it slows us down instead of speeding us up?"

She mentioned, a few evenings later, over dinner at her parents' house, that she had brought up the idea of making the business more digital. Her father, who had started the company in the late '80s with a single borrowed lathe, put down his steel tumbler and said

"When I switched from handwritten ledgers to printed invoices, people laughed at me," he said. "But that step won us bigger clients because they took us more seriously. If you want the company to last another thirty years, you must prepare it for people who have never met you, investors, analysts, shareholders."

Her younger brother, an IT consultant in Chennai, added, "Digital systems don't replace your control. They make it visible so others can trust it without walking into this factory."

The following week, Anitha called her CA, a merchant banker, and Murugan to the conference room. They mapped the essentials for IPO readiness on a whiteboard:

Murugan frowned. "Madam, if a client wants to know about an urgent part, I just call the store. Why complicate it?"

The banker replied, "Because in three years, it won't just be clients asking. It will be market regulators and institutional investors. If you can show them accurate numbers quickly, you're proving you can handle growth without chaos."

That made Murugan quiet.

Starting Small, Thinking Big, Seek Help

Instead of starting with automation, ERP software, etc., Anitha outlined a plan to assess her company's current state and determine what it would take to reach the IPO level. The people, process, culture, skill level, regulations, and numerous other points or enablers were broken down into stages.

Initially, what looked easy to her started becoming complex and overwhelming and too much for a single person to solve. She realised she needed more people to join the brainstorming process, as well as consultants with a proven track record who had done this earlier.

The aim was simple: to make the best parts of their system visible, consistent, and easy to verify, without changing everything, and to achieve this with experts and their expertise. The IPO would take her business to the next level, and the control, responsibility, and transparency would bring a new level of significance. It won't remain the same; is she, the team, and the organisation ready for that leap?

Six months later, in the thick of the pre-festival rush for weaving industry upgrades, an urgent email came from a long-standing European client. They wanted twice their usual order, and they liked it in twelve days.

Three years ago, that would have caused frantic phone calls, supervisors running between departments, and files being pulled from dusty cabinets.

This time, Anitha called a short meeting on the shop floor. The production log showed machine availability instantly. The system flagged a shortage of a key alloy; the purchasing team placed the order within an hour, attaching last year's quality certificate from the archive so the vendor could dispatch immediately.

Midway through the job, the client requested inspection records from a similar batch eight months earlier. Murugan typed in the part number, filtered by date, and sent the report in minutes.

On day ten, the shipment inspector arrived. Every delivery note, invoice, and quality check document was already in a single digital folder. No missing papers. No rewrites.

When the last crate was sealed, Anitha stood by the bay door watching it roll out. "Three years ago," she said quietly, "we might have lost this order. Today, we finished two days early."

With this, she became more determined to let's go IPO. The next was a hunt for a consultant, bankers, advisors and a lot more. She had some doubts and apprehensions, but her strong faith seemed to be fighting all the odds.

Reflection

For Anitha, the first step toward IPO readiness was not a software purchase; it was a shift in perspective. Going digital wasn't about replacing her instincts or her control; it was about making them visible and reliable to people she'd never meet in person.

She still walks the factory floor every morning, greeting each worker by name, but she now knows that the systems she has built will stand up to the scrutiny of auditors and analysts. The IPO may still be three years away, but the discipline it demands is already part of the company's daily rhythm.

The Matrix that can help

The matrix only highlights the digital aspects of IPO. Going IPO requires a lot of other pieces fitting together. Anitha's thought process serves as a starting point, and then we work with the ecosystem and providers.

2x2 Matrix: Relevance of Technology for SME IPO in India

	Easy to Implement	Complex to Implement
High Impact	**Quick Wins** - Automate compliance reporting - E-invoicing & GST e-filing integration - Bank reconciliation tools - Payroll & statutory compliance software - Automated expense management	**Strategic Must-haves** - ERP integration across finance, sales, and production - Supply chain traceability with vendor portals - Board reporting dashboards & KPI trackers - CRM integrated with sales pipeline forecasting - Business continuity & disaster recovery systems
Low Impact	**Low Priority** - Niche analytics tools for small process areas - Experimental AR/VR showroom or product demo - Social media sentiment analytics (unless brand-heavy) - Gamified employee engagement platforms	**Long-term Differentiators** - AI forecasting for demand & production - Blockchain smart contracts for vendor & client deals - IoT-enabled quality control & predictive maintenance - Digital twins for production lines - ESG tracking & reporting platforms

Chapter 39: The Cost of Authenticity

"The biggest risk is not taking any risk. In a world that is changing very quickly, the only strategy that is guaranteed to fail is not taking risks."

- *Mark Zuckerberg*

The sun-drenched lanes of Jaipur's old city carry a history not just in their architecture but in the very air. Here, the aroma is a rich, layered tapestry of jasmine from a vendor's cart, sweet cardamom from a chai stall, and, strongest of all, the deep, unmistakable scent of pure, unadulterated leather. Inside a small, unassuming shop, the gentle clink of a hammer on a needle is a sound as old as the city itself. The walls are a gallery of family photos, each one showing a generation of men bent over the same workbench, their hands creating art from hide. This is where Mr. Alok Singh, a man in his early sixties with a trimmed moustache and a calm, knowing smile, runs "Jaipur Juttis."

His business is a living testament to the dying art of hand-stitched footwear. Mr. Singh is a master craftsman, his hands weathered and strong, each line a story of an intricate stitch or a perfect finish. His grandfather had started the shop, and his father had handed him the tools, not as a profession, but as a sacred trust. He and his small team of artisans don't just make shoes; they create heirlooms. "We have been making juttis for three generations," he said to me, his voice as measured as his movements. "We use a specific thread, a specific needle. Every pair takes weeks. Our customers come back because they know this. This is our value. This is our promise."

He gestured to an extensive, glossy catalogue on the counter, a modern tool that seemed utterly out of place. "A big e-commerce company in Delhi called me. They want to put my products online," he began, a frown settling on his face. "My nephew says it's the future. He says we will reach millions of people. But tell me, how will a photo on a screen show the hours of work in a single stitch? How will it convey the smell of the leather? How will it feel the difference between a shoe made with love and one made by a machine? Digital is for selling things, for sure. But my product is not just an item. It is a craft. I fear that if I put my juttis next to a thousand others, made by machines and sold at half the price, my value will be lost. I want to be seen as a traditional brand. Digital will kill that positioning. It will flatten my soul."

His apprehension wasn't a lack of ambition; it was a fierce, protective instinct for the very soul of his business. He saw digital as a homogenising force, a soulless sea where his handcrafted masterpieces would be reduced to a generic product code and a low price tag. He wasn't against progress; he was a guardian of his legacy, and he was terrified that the online marketplace would turn his art into a mere commodity, indistinguishable from the rest. The idea of competing on price was an insult to his family's name. His father had taught him that the most valuable thing an artisan can sell is his integrity. How could he sell integrity on a screen?

The Two-Part Digital Strategy: A Lesson in Storytelling

His niece, Priya, a young design graduate with a passion for her family's heritage, had been listening from the back. She understood her uncle's fear completely. She knew the value was not in the jutti itself, but in the story of its creation. She walked over, a small, hopeful smile on her face. "Uncle," she said softly, "what if digital is not just for selling? What if it's for telling our story?"

She proposed a different kind of digital strategy, one that didn't just sell but also preserved and amplified the very essence of their brand. The strategy was built on two simple, powerful pillars.

The first step was to move the focus from the product to the process. They would not simply post a picture of a jutti with a price tag. They would use digital media to document and narrate the story of its creation. Priya began with her phone, filming the artisans at work with the eye of an artist. She captured the careful, rhythmic tapping of the hammer, the painstaking detail of a needle pulling through layers of fabric and leather. She focused on the weathered hands of the master craftsman, showing the wisdom in every movement. She started a new Instagram account and a simple, one-page website. The content was not a sales pitch; it was a mini-documentary. One video showed a close-up of a worker carefully embroidering a single peacock feather. The caption read, "Each feather takes two hours of hand-stitching. This is the difference. This is our tradition."

Priya's approach was about creating a sense of connection. The videos felt intimate and authentic, a direct line from the artisan to the customer. They were not just selling a shoe; they were inviting customers to witness the soul of the craft. They also started a weekly "Handmade with Love" series on Instagram, where Mr. Singh would talk about the history of a specific pattern or the type of leather used. It was a simple idea, yet powerful.

The second step was to create a curated digital shopfront. Mr. Singh was right to be wary of large e-commerce platforms. Competing on price with mass-produced footwear would be a losing battle. Instead, Priya used a basic platform to create a small, exclusive online shop. The products were limited, the images were high-resolution, and the descriptions told a story. "Hand-stitched by our master artisan, this piece is inspired by the gardens of Jaipur's Amber Fort." The website also included a "Meet Our Artisans" section, featuring photos and brief bios of the craftsmen, which put a face to the name of the brand. It was a digital space that felt as warm and intimate as their physical shop.

The Return: From Hidden Costs to Measurable Value

The results of this strategy appeared almost immediately. The returns were not measured in a sudden spike in sales, but in a profound shift in perception and reputation.

- **Amplified Authenticity:** The digital storytelling didn't kill the brand's value; it made it more visible than ever before. Within weeks, the Instagram videos received hundreds of likes and comments from a global audience. Customers from as far away as Bangalore and the UK sent messages asking about the craftsmanship. One comment read, "I would gladly pay more for something that is handmade with this much care. This is true luxury." Another wrote, "Thank you for sharing this. It makes me feel connected to the art." The digital presence had not commoditised the product; it had elevated it. It had shown that "traditional" could also be "premium." The narrative of the artisan was a powerful counter-narrative to the cheap, mass-produced digital landscape.

- **Targeted Growth:** The business gained a new, highly-engaged audience. These were not customers looking for the cheapest pair of shoes. They were buyers who specifically valued quality, heritage, and the story behind a product. They found a small, loyal, and global customer base that was willing to pay a fair price for the craft. The digital efforts brought them the "right" kind of business, ensuring they could grow without compromising their values. They weren't fighting on price; they were winning on value.

- **Preservation of Craft:** The digital archive became more than a marketing tool; it was a living document of their family's legacy. It was a way to document and preserve the traditional process for future generations. Mr. Singh, who had always worried about his craft dying out, now saw a path to its preservation through digital media. The digital footprint was a promise to the future, a way to attract new, young talent who could see the worth and a way to honour the work of the artisans for posterity.

Months later, Mr. Singh showed me his online shop. He smiled, pointing to a pair of intricately embroidered juttis. "That one was sold to a customer in Singapore. She messaged me with a question about the stitch, and I sent her a photo of my uncle working on a similar pair. She wrote back, 'Thank you for sharing your story. I will treasure these.'"

He closed the laptop and looked up. "I was wrong," he admitted. "I thought digital was only for speed and cheap prices. I was afraid it would turn my craft into an item. But Priya showed me something important: digital is a tool. It doesn't have its own value. Its value is in how you use it to tell your own story. My father's customers knew our story because they sat in this shop and drank tea with him. Now, people all over the world can see our story, and they can choose to value it. Digital didn't kill my tradition. It gave it a new voice." His fear was replaced by a quiet pride, a confidence that his legacy was no longer confined to the narrow lanes of Jaipur.

Mini-Framework: Digital Marketing for Traditional Businesses

- **Focus on the "Why":** Don't just show the product. Show the process, the people, the history, and the purpose behind it. Digital is an excellent medium for storytelling.

- **Curate, Don't Compete:** Avoid competing on large e-commerce sites where price is the only factor. Instead, create your own small, curated digital space that reflects your brand's unique value.

- **Embrace Exclusivity:** Use digital to create a sense of exclusivity. Limited editions, behind-the-scenes content, and personalised interactions can make your brand feel unique and valuable.

- **Turn Content into a Legacy:** Use digital platforms not just for sales, but as a way to document, preserve, and share the knowledge of your craft for generations to come.

Reflection

Mr. Alok Singh's apprehension was a common and valid one for any business with a strong, traditional identity. The fear that a digital world obsessed with speed and volume would devalue their craftsmanship was a real and powerful deterrent. But his experience showed that digital is not a single, monolithic force. It is a tool, and its impact is entirely dependent on how it is wielded. By using digital media not just to sell, but to tell his story, he didn't just find new customers; he found a new way to honour his legacy. The digital space, when used with intent, became a powerful ally, a guardian of his tradition, and a beacon for others who value authenticity.

He learned that a digital presence, when authentic and intentional, can add a new layer of value to a traditional brand. It can connect with a global audience on a personal level, build trust through transparency, and ultimately command a premium price. The ROI of his digital investment was not just in sales, but in the preservation of his craft and the strengthening of his brand's reputation for generations to come. He didn't lose his position; he cemented it. His niece, Priya, just needed a nudge and support to help her uncle. She knew the way, but convincing her uncle was tough; she got the support through me, and here it is. At times, people just need a nudge and a spark to transform something, especially a legacy; it's tough, but it happens.

Section 6: The Digital Mindset & Future Readiness

The final leap is mindset. Once MSMEs begin their digital journey, the challenge is to keep up with change, embrace reviews, deal with the chaos of growth, and stay open to innovations like Artificial Intelligence. Digital is not just about tools; it's about thinking differently, being agile, and preparing for the future. This closing section leaves readers not just less afraid of digital, but excited about where it can take them.

Chapter 40: Visibility Without Volume

"In the world of business, the people who are most visible often become the most valuable."

- *Robin Sharma*

It was the kind of afternoon when even the fans seemed tired. In Bhilwara's old market, most shops had their shutters halfway down to keep the heat out. But one shop was still open — Shree Ganesh Stationers. Tucked between a paan stall and a tailor's shop, it stood quietly, like it always had.

Inside, Gopal Jain sat behind the counter, hunched over a thick ledger, carefully doing his daily totals in neat, squared-off writing.

"Slow day?" I asked, stepping in and glancing at the empty front area.

"Off-season," he replied, not looking up. "Wait till next month. Schools reopen. Then you'll see."

The shop had the air of something time had respected. Wooden shelves stretched from floor to ceiling, filled with every kind of school supply — registers, chart paper, geometry boxes, maps rolled up in bundles, and rows of labelled files. It was clear that this was more than just a shop; it was a place generations had come to with lists scribbled on notebook paper.

After a few minutes, I asked, "Have you ever thought of putting the shop online? Just a simple listing or a few posts on WhatsApp during school season?"

He gave a soft laugh and shook his head. "People don't come here because of ads. They come because they know me. You ask anyone in this colony where to buy stationery, and they'll send you here. Word of mouth is enough."

There was no arrogance in his tone — only quiet confidence. After all, this shop had served families for over twenty-five years. For him, the idea of promoting it online felt unnecessary, even distracting.

When Familiarity Feels Safer Than Visibility

"Of course," I said. "There's no replacement for loyal customers. But what about new ones? Families who've just moved in, or that coaching centre that opened near the temple—do they know about your shop?"

He paused, just briefly. "I guess not. But if they need chart paper, they'll ask around."

I nodded. "They might. Or they might search for 'stationery near me.' And if your name doesn't show up, they won't skip you because they don't like you. They'll skip you because they never knew you were there."

He looked thoughtful for a moment. "I always thought all this digital stuff was for big stores. The ones with home delivery and fancy packaging."

"It can be," I replied. "But it doesn't have to be. You don't have to offer delivery or discounts. Just show what you already have so people who need it can find you."

He didn't say yes. But he didn't shut the door either.

A Small Step Toward Digital

Later that day, I assisted Gopal Ji in creating a simple Google Business listing. We added a few pictures — the front of the shop, the counter stacked with registers, the shelf full of model-making kits. His son helped pin the exact location.

"No schemes," he reminded me. "And no shouting. I'm not putting up blinking offers."

"No need," I said. "Just be easy to find."

Three weeks later, my phone buzzed with a message.

"Someone came today asking for a model-making kit," he wrote. "He said he saw the photo online. Didn't even ask for a discount."

He sent another message a few minutes later.

"I think we'll post our school reopening stock on WhatsApp next week. Just to see."

He was as happy and excited as a kid when they got something new to play around with. Since it was free, he didn't mind trying. I am sure that in the future, he will explore other free tools and, gradually, perhaps a few paid ones as well.

Deep down, I was also afraid that since it was his first experience with digital, he might be cautious and not go overboard. I revisited his shop and congratulated him on taking the first step, which was not going live on the listing but rather considering its potential benefits for his business.

He looked at me with a smile in his eyes and thanked me for this simple yet effective tool. He confessed to searching his shop on Google multiple times and also sharing his business profile listing with all his relatives and friends. I could sense the same happiness when someone gets published in a newspaper for a good reason, and they keep telling everyone about it. Rightly so. It was a significant first step.

I informed him about the Do's and Don'ts of online safety, emphasising the importance of not sharing any confidential information.

What Digital-First Really Means

A digital-first mindset doesn't mean forgetting the people who already walk in. It means making space for the ones who haven't met you yet. It's not about changing how you run your shop. It's about allowing new doors to open.

For Gopal ji, nothing changed inside his shop. The ledger was still on the counter. The pencils were still sorted by brand. The conversations still started with "What do you want?" But outside his shop, something shifted. He had become visible.

While I was sipping my evening cup of tea, I thought, 'How can I create a simple approach that can help many Gopal Jis take the first step to get found in the digital market, especially the local ones who know how to deal with it?'

"SAATHI" Approach for Digital-First Thinking

- **S – Show:** Use real, simple photos of your shop and items on Google/WhatsApp/Facebook/Other platforms; no need for filters or flashy design.
- **A – Awareness:** Understand why going digital matters for visibility, not just marketing. Know that "digital-first" doesn't replace your shop; it amplifies it.
- **A – Authenticity:** Stick to your shop's values with no false promises or unrealistic offers. Be real; be consistent.

- **T – Trust:** Ask known and loyal customers to leave honest reviews or testimonials on your website or social media platforms. It builds credibility for new buyers.
- **H – Habit:** Post at least one update a week, such as seasonal stock, new arrivals, or a shop photo. Regularity keeps your business top of mind.
- **I – Inquiry:** Ask walk-in customers how they found you. Track online visibility and refine based on feedback.

Reflection

Gopal Ji didn't change how he greeted his customers or the way he arranged his files. He allowed his shop to be seen by someone who wouldn't have found it otherwise. And in a world that is increasingly online, sometimes being seen is all it takes to grow.

He didn't shift away from the footfall. He gave it another path to reach him.

Closing Thought

You don't need to advertise to everyone. But you do need to be found by the right ones.

Chapter 41: Looms and Likes: Digital Means Visible

"If you're not on the internet, then you don't exist."

— *Seth Godin*

The sun was still soft over the pine ridges as I wound my way into a small hillside locality near Shillong, Meghalaya. The roads narrowed, but every bend opened into a view of quiet homes and sloping gardens. I was headed to meet Iakop Nongrum, a second-generation artisan who ran Banrap Collection, a family initiative renowned for its handwoven shawls dyed in vibrant colours such as turmeric, indigo, and charcoal.

The entrance to his workshop was modest, marked only by a bamboo sign and a faded hand-painted logo. Inside, the smell of natural dyes mingled with steam from the tea kettle. Several women sat on backstrap looms, weaving in almost meditative silence.

Iakop welcomed me in. A tall man with gentle eyes and turmeric-stained fingers, he looked like someone who had worked every corner of his business, from sourcing threads to shipping parcels.

Over two cups of strong red tea, he spoke openly.

"We work hard. Our quality is good. But when I search for 'Meghalaya handlooms' online, I see influencers from Mumbai showing off shawls we wove. They get the likes. We stay invisible."

I paused before answering. "And how does that make you feel?"

He gave a half-smile. "I feel like the world listens to loud voices, not real ones. It's like my father used to say, a good tree doesn't shout about its shade."

The Dilemma of Digital Silence

He wasn't the only one.

In Agra, a leatherworker named Muneer told me, "My hands are cracked from years of work. However, people tend to trust a photo more than a person. If I get one bad review, they don't call again."

In Kozhikode, Kerala, I met Salma, who sold homemade pickles. Her neighbour once took a picture of her jars, posted it on Instagram with a recipe caption, and suddenly had more followers and more orders.

"She's not wrong," Salma said. "But I was too shy to post mine. I didn't think anyone cared."

These were not people chasing fame. They were protectors of the craft. And yet, the fear of being misunderstood online was intense.

The Turning Point: From Silence to Story

I asked Iakop, "Tell me what your regular customers say."

He laughed softly. "They say it smells like their grandmother's closet. They say it reminds them of weddings, winter mornings, and old hill songs."

"That's your story," I said. "Not marketing. Not hype. Just memory and meaning."

We started with a small step. A feedback journal on the counter, no instructions, just a pen and a note: *Share your thoughts.*

Within a week, three notes came in. One said, *"Reminds me of my mother's shawl, lost long ago."* Another said, *"Please don't ever change the smell of this place."*

His niece, Amika, a college student home for the holidays, took a photo of a note and posted it on Instagram.

No filters. Just a photo of the paper with the loom in the background.

That post got 312 likes.

Not viral. But real.

Responding, Not Reacting

They created a simple Google listing next. One tourist left a three-star review complaining about the steep walk.

Iakop was unsure at first. "Should I respond? Or just ignore it?"

"Respond like a host," I said. "Thank them. Offer to guide them next time. Show grace."

He did. A day later, the reviewer replied: *"Thank you. I'd still visit again, this time with better shoes."*

The interaction mattered more than the rating.

From Invisible to Intentional

In Bhopal, I visited a bakery run by two brothers, Deepak and Nishant. For 90 days, they posted one photo daily on WhatsApp Status and Instagram Stories. Not polished shots. Just daily bakes, handwritten labels, occasional spills.

By the third month, a local food blogger posted about them. Orders doubled that week.

"We didn't change anything," Deepak told me. "We just showed up online like we do in real life."

A New Kind of Marketplace

In Imphal, a bamboo crafts collective began using WhatsApp to answer questions from tourists. In Jaipur, a block-print studio printed customer reviews and taped them near the entrance.

One said, *"I didn't buy anything, but I left feeling inspired."* That line became their website headline.

The digital world is not always about algorithms. Sometimes, it's just about being available when someone is searching.

Reputation Isn't Built by Reviews. It's Revealed by Response.

When I returned to Shillong after three months, I found a printed banner outside Banrap Collection. It read: *"Our hands wove this. Your words carry it forward."*

Inside, Iakop told me, "We still get fewer likes than the big stores. However, now that people find us, they already know us. They come for the story. They stay for the shawl."

He showed me a review that said: *"My heart slowed down in this place."*

That, he said, was the best five-star they could hope for.

Mini Framework: Digital Presence That Reflects You

Concern	Steps to Take	Why It Works
Fear of negative reviews	Respond with honesty and humility	Shows character and openness
Feeling judged by likes or ranking	Focus on sharing real stories from your team and customers.	Builds emotional connection beyond numbers
No tech-savvy staff	Involve the next generation or neighbours who understand digital basics	Bridges the gap without hiring big agencies
Unsure where to start	Begin with a Google listing, basic photos, and a WhatsApp share routine	Starts momentum without cost

Reflection

Visibility doesn't come from volume. It comes from value.

Marketing for small businesses is not about shouting or working less. Ultimately, your work will be judged on the hard work and the excellent product you create or the services you deliver. However, online, likes and shares, etc., amplify your work, help you understand what your customers and market want, and make you visible to those who are unaware of your work and may be looking for your craft. Get discovered, be visible online.

It's not about boasting your work, but rather showcasing your craft with the same enthusiasm you display over the counter, at your shop, or in front of your customers. It is storytelling. And storytelling is not a skill you learn online. It's a truth you live and choose to share.

Whether it's a shawl in Shillong, a pickle in Kozhikode, or a cake in Bhopal, it all begins when you stop worrying about being famous and start focusing on being found by the right people.

Chapter 42: "There are scams everywhere."

"The greatest weapon against fraud is information."
— Frank Abagnale **(former con artist turned FBI advisor, "Catch Me If You Can")**

Mr. Bashir owned a modest yet bustling mobile recharge and accessories shop tucked into a busy commercial bylane of Aligarh.. His outlet was bigger than the rest—two display tables, two helpers, and a storeroom filled with boxes of cables, SIM cards, and used phones.

From a cursory glance, he appeared to be digital-savvy. He took UPI payments, had a simple billing app, and even made festival offers in local WhatsApp groups.

But when I lightly suggested broadening his use of technology—building a simple online business page and employing a verified CRM program for frequent customer follow-up—He interrupted, his tone curt and final..

"Don't speak to me about new digital applications," he said. "I've already witnessed what occurs."

A Story That Shattered His Trust

He unfolded a folding chair and sat down.

"Last year," he explained, "my friend Zaheer, who owns the large electrical store opposite the bus stand, received a visit from a man purporting to be from a digital firm. He was dressed properly, with an ID card, laptop, and printed brochure. Told him he was providing a premium listing in a new business app. Guaranteed targeted visibility, cashback promotions, and improved UPI tools."

Zaheer paid ₹7,000 for the listing.

The app never worked," Bashir said, frustration creeping into his voice.. "And within a few weeks, even the payment company would not respond. The guy's number was wrong. Vanished.

Zaheer complained, but no one responded. He was too embarrassed to speak about it afterwards.

"I still remember how embarrassed he looked. Ever since then, I do not trust anyone who comes in with a tech idea."

I acknowledged his fear, not with dismissal, but with understanding.

Bashir bhai, you are perfectly right to be suspicious. You're not alone, these scams have occurred to companies all over India."

"But just as one bad parts supplier isn't going to make all your distributors crooked, one flawed app isn't going to make digital itself the issue."

He nodded slowly. "So how am I supposed to know what's safe and trustworthy?"

We navigated through his phone together:

I demonstrated to him how to verify if an app is officially listed on the NPCI (National Payments Corporation of India) or RBI-approved platforms, how to review developer details, user ratings, and authorisations before installing, and why apps must be downloaded always from Google Play Store or the App Store, not through forwarded links or generic websites

We discussed what proper onboarding entails—customer support channels, privacy policies, and apparent brand identity.

I also mentioned details of digital security workshops organised by local NGOs and government institutions for micro, small, and medium-sized business owners, particularly those involved in trading and retail.

"They spell these things out in simple language," I told him. "No sales talk. Just protection."

He arched an eyebrow. "Can I send my employees too?"

"Even better," I said. "Make them your first line of defence."

Bashir's experience is not an exception. A 2023 survey by DSCI found that nearly 38% of small Indian businesses reported being targeted by digital fraud at least once. Now, this number has increased significantly. Trust isn't just built on tech; it's built on transparency, training, and tools.

The Shift: From Distrust to Discipline

Later that week, Bashir phoned me.

"I enrolled in a government-recognised UPI app tied to my business account," he explained. "No agents. I did your checklist."

He also developed a new store internal policy:

- Only he and one trusted employee could use digital tools

- No payments accepted without SMS or app approval

- Weekly digital review meetings to catch mistakes early

He even posted the Digital Trust Checklist on paper and taped it to the back of his counter.

Now I feel like I'm in control," he said to me. "Not afraid. Just aware."

Bashir's Digital Trust Checklist

A trusted tool for businesses to remain secure:

- Only use RBI/NPCI-approved apps

- Download from only official app stores

- Check the developer name and reviews on the Play or App Store

- Never click on spam links

- Never give away your OTP, PIN, or passwords

- Activate two-factor authentication

- Educate employees on basic digital hygiene

- Maintain emergency contact for escalation of disputes (bank helpline, UPI portal).

- Request company registration and GSTIN, etc., and verify on the government website.

- Take a photo of the agent ID and cross-check online

- Insist on an official email confirmation of product features explained or promises

- Ask for a few local references or people the company has worked with, and get their feedback before making the payment

- If it's a substantial amount, consider getting into an agreement..

"You may feel that all this sounds like too much work or unnecessary caution. But believe me, regret is far more expensive than discipline. I've been a victim of a scam too. That's precisely why I'm writing this book: so others like you don't have to learn the hard way."

Closing Thought

One scam may cost money.

But uncontrolled fear may cost growth.

The solution is not withdrawal—it's wisdom.

Bashir's journey wasn't about mastering software. It was about reclaiming agency in a space that had once betrayed him.

Chapter 43: The Digital Maestro

"If we teach today's students as we taught yesterday's, we rob them of tomorrow."

- John Dewey

Mr Goswami's classroom in Rishikesh, Uttarakhand, was a testament to his three decades of teaching. He believed in a profound simplicity of education: a guru, a student, and a blackboard. His success was not built on a website but on word-of-mouth, on the tangible results of his students and the trust of their parents. For Mr Goswami, learning was a profoundly human endeavour, a process that thrived in the quiet presence of a mentor. This was his business, built not on code, but on character. He began his days with the familiar ritual of wiping the blackboard clean, a gesture that symbolised a fresh start for both him and his students. His classes were a blend of rigorous mathematical problem-solving and philosophical discussions, punctuated by his unique, patient style. Parents knew him. Students revered him. His method was timeless, or so he believed.

Lately, however, an unseen anxiety had begun to creep into his classroom. It was fuelled by a competitor, a new tutorial centre down the road, which, despite having less experienced teachers, was attracting more students with a futuristic-sounding "Artificial Intelligence (AI) driven personalised curriculum." Mr Goswami's apprehension was not just about their content; it was about his own inability to master their tools. "What is this AI? So many new tools are coming out daily, and the prompt: I cannot master it?" he lamented to his young assistant, Arjun, a former student he had mentored since childhood. He saw AI as a betrayal of his craft, a threat to the integrity of education, and believed its rapid pace made it impossible to keep up with.

The Real-World Crisis: Beyond the Classroom Walls

The problem did not arrive as a drop in his students' grades. It came as a more profound crisis of trust, affordability, and academic integrity. His business, once a beacon of stability, was showing signs of stagnation. The number of new student registrations remained flat, and the latest, tech-forward competitor was quietly poaching his most promising students. The true catalyst for change came during a series of unsettling meetings with parents, whose concerns went far beyond convenience.

"Your teaching is excellent, sir," one parent, a government employee, began, his tone respectful yet firm. "But the other place gives us an app to see our child's progress in real-time. And they say their AI knows exactly what my child is struggling with. It sounds... expensive. Can we trust them with our children's data? I read an article about a data breach at a big ed-tech company. It makes me very nervous." This question struck at the heart of Mr Goswami's deepest fears. He knew nothing about data privacy and worried about the financial burden of adopting a complex, high-cost tech system, a common barrier for MSMEs. He tried to reassure her with his years of experience, but he could see her concern was not about his ability, but about her child's digital safety.

A second parent, a local shopkeeper, highlighted a different, equally pressing issue. "My son has to travel to another town to use a computer. The other centre's system seems to require a lot of expensive hardware. We can't afford that, and honestly, not all our children have access to a good internet connection at home." This fear perfectly captured the real-world challenge of the digital divide that persists across India, where technology is not a universal luxury. Mr Goswami had never considered this, assuming that every family had the same access.

The final blow came when a third parent, a lawyer, expressed a fear that felt existential. "With all this AI-generated content, how can we be sure our children are actually learning and not just copying? What happens to their critical thinking and their ability to write their own thoughts? They say AI can generate essays and solve complex math problems. It feels like this new technology is making it easy for them to cheat." Mr Goswami's heart sank. These were not just technical problems; they were fundamental issues of academic integrity and social equity, real fears that threatened the very fabric of his business. He realised that his inability to articulate how his "human" qualities addressed these issues was costing him not just revenue, but also the community's trust.

Digital-First Mindset: Amplifying Wisdom, Not Replacing It

Arjun, the young mentee, understood that his mentor's apprehension was not about technology but about preserving his values. He did not ask him to learn coding or "master AI." Instead, he introduced a fundamental shift in thinking: the digital-first mindset. "Sir," he said, "you do not need to master the tool to use it. You already have the wisdom. The digital part is just a way to make your wisdom scalable." He explained that AI was not a replacement for his profound knowledge, but a way to amplify it, addressing the systemic issues that were holding the business back. This was the digital-first mindset in its most pragmatic form.

They applied this mindset to the tutorial centre, leveraging a new generation of AI tools designed to be both powerful and empathetic, which directly addressed the core challenges of their business.

1. Present Issue: Tedious Administration & Communication Gaps

- The Problem: Mr Goswami spent countless hours manually tracking attendance, calling parents, and sending out reminders for fees and class schedules. This was a massive drain on his time, preventing him from focusing on his primary role: teaching.

- The Solution: Arjun set up a low-cost, automated system using a combination of Google Forms and Zapier (or a similar no-code automation tool). He created a simple Google Form for daily attendance, which his assistant could fill out in seconds. An automated "Zap" was set up to trigger a daily SMS to parents if their child was marked as absent. The same system sent automated fee reminders with a secure payment link, saving countless hours of manual work and ensuring transparent, timely communication. This was technology working for him, not against him.

2. Present Issue: Financial Burden & The Digital Divide

- The Problem: The fear of expensive software and the reality of unequal access to technology.

- The Solution: Instead of a costly, data-hungry app, they built the entire system on a combination of low-cost, widely accessible platforms. The automated communication was based on SMS, which works on any mobile phone. For academic tracking, they used a simple, secure cloud-based form accessible via a simple web link that parents could fill out. A student could access a learning module or quiz from an old smartphone and get a prompt-based question via a simple text message, eliminating the need for expensive hardware. This approach directly addressed the financial and accessibility issues, making quality education available to a broader segment of the community.

3. Future-Proofing: Personalised Learning at Scale & Predictive Analysis

- The Problem: Mr Goswami's greatest strength was identifying student weaknesses, but this was a manual, time-consuming process that did not scale.

- The Solution: They used Google Forms for all quizzes. The data was automatically sent to a Google Sheet. Arjun then connected this sheet to a business intelligence tool. With a few clicks, they created a real-time dashboard showing Mr Goswami which students were struggling with which specific concepts. For example, if a student consistently made mistakes on problems involving a particular concept like trigonometry, the dashboard would flag it, allowing Mr Goswami to offer proactive, targeted help, a truly personalised curriculum that no human could achieve at scale. The AI was not teaching; it was a powerful diagnostic tool for the master.

4. Future-Proofing: Academic Integrity in the Age of Generative AI

- The Problem: The fear of plagiarism and the loss of genuine learning.

- The Solution: To address the plagiarism issue, they leveraged a dynamic AI content generator. Mr Goswami began using free, powerful AI assistants to create unique and context-specific practice questions. He would provide the AI with a specific learning objective, and it would generate new problems that required genuine critical thinking and problem-solving, not just memorisation. The assignments were constantly changing, making it impossible for a student to copy answers from a textbook or a static online solution. They realised the best way to fight the misuse of a tool was to master its proper use.

The Transformation: From Master to Proactive Partner

The relationship between the mentor and mentee evolved from a traditional one into a collaborative partnership. Mr Goswami, initially sceptical, began to see the value. He would watch as Arjun showed him a dashboard flagging a student who was predicted to struggle with a particular topic. "This," Arjun explained, "is the algorithm of your wisdom, sir. It's just making your intuition visible and verifiable." He realised that the digital tools were not a replacement for his wisdom; they were a vessel to deliver it more efficiently and widely. He learned that the "wisdom of the prompt" was simply about knowing the right question to ask a tool to solve a problem.

The digital approach led to a transformation. New student registrations began to pour in, as parents were impressed by the seamless communication and personalised learning. The business, once stagnant, began to grow again, and Mr Goswami found himself with more time to dedicate to the one-on-one connections that made him a great teacher. He saw that his expertise, once confined to his classroom, could now reach customers across the city and beyond. The digital world was not a threat to his physical craft; it was its most powerful ally, solving real-world problems and future-proofing his legacy.

Mini-Framework: Digital for Real-World Problems

- Problem-First, Tool-Second: Do not adopt a tool because it is new. Identify a real, tangible business problem (e.g., a communication gap, manual data entry, lack of trust) and then find a simple digital solution for it.

- Privacy by Design: For any business handling personal data, prioritise solutions that guarantee privacy from the ground up, such as localised data processing. This builds trust and sets you apart from the competition.

- Enhance, Not Replace: Use AI to handle the mundane, repeatable tasks, like data entry, scheduling, or generating basic content. This frees you up to focus on the human-centric aspects of your business, which is your real unique selling proposition.

- Embrace the Low-Cost Stack: Modern, powerful tools do not have to be expensive. By leveraging platforms like simple email/SMS services, cloud-based forms, and other freemium services, you can build a robust digital presence without significant capital investment.

- Future-Proof with Data: Even simple digital tools can generate data. Use this data, visualised in a dashboard, to gain insights and predict future needs, allowing you to stay ahead of the curve and offer proactive solutions.

Reflection

Mr Goswami's journey is a powerful case study for any MSME that feels overwhelmed by the rapid pace of technological change. His fear was valid; the speed of AI innovation can seem impossible to keep up with. But he discovered that the solution was not to become a master of a new tool, but to adopt a new mindset. His expertise, with the aid of able support, which was once confined to his classroom, could now reach a wider audience. The digital became his ally, solving his problems and future-proofing his legacy.

www.ingramcontent.com/pod-product-compliance
Lightning Source LLC
Chambersburg PA
CBHW021920190326
41519CB00009B/856